fatale

HOW FRENCH
WOMEN DO IT

Edith Kunz

Bridgewood Press

Third Printing, December 2006

Bridgewood Press,
4610 North 40th Street, Phoenix, AZ 85018 U.S.A.

Book and cover design, Jennifer Therieau

Cover art: François Boucher, Nude on a Sofa (Reclining Girl),
1752, oil on canvas, Pinakothek at Munich.

ISBN 0-927015-25-0
Library of Congress Card Number 00-131734
Printed in the United States of America

To my mother

CONTENTS

how french women do it

et's face it, a French woman's face is not her fortune. Madame du Barry, Madame Recamier, Brigitte Bardot and Catherine Denueve are among the exceptions; however, the usual line-up of fascinating Gallic damsels would never qualify on the runway of today's beauty contests. Josephine Bonaparte, Madame Maintenon, Sarah Bernhardt, Edith Piaf, Colette, Simone de Beauvoir, and Jeanne Moreau have much more behind their captivating seductiveness than ever meets the eye. Just what is the secret to the mystifying allure that surrounds the French femme fatale?

"One is not born a woman, one becomes one."

Simone de Beauvoir
(1908-86)

Throughout a glorious and colorful heritage which reads like a dramatic adventure story, Frenchwomen have used feminine cunning and innate charm to wield tremendous power in a land historically governed by men. Officially only kings and male heirs were allowed to sit on the throne of France, but even after the last king was overthrown more than a hundred years ago and France became a democracy, men continued to occupy the position of chief executive.

Official titles, however, fail to tell the whole story concerning where the power lies among the French hierarchy. One must read between the lines of the long list of French kings, emperors and presidents to gain insight into the mysterious undercurrent of influence constantly flowing from the country's female population.

History books are laden with names of French mavens who greatly influenced the course of state affairs while occupying no official office. Saint

"There is no such thing as great talent without great willpower."

Honoré de Balzac (1799-1850)

Genevieve and her army saved the city of Paris from Atilla The Hun in 451 A.D. and today she is revered as the city's patron saint. The wife of King Louis VII, Eleanor of Aquitaine, led crusades to the Holy Land in the 12th Century. Joan of Arc headed a legion which drove out the English invaders in 1430 and put Charles VII back on the French throne. Diane de Poitiers, Madame de Maintenon, Madame du Barry and Madame du Pompadour were but a few famous mistresses who made great use of their superior status in the king's bedchamber to acquire extraordinary political clout.

In the Middle Ages, Eleanor of Aquitane, the only daughter of the enormously wealthy Duke of Poitou, had impressive energy and intellectual charms which she put into play by marrying not one, but two kings, first Louis VII of France and then Henry II of England. King Louis was devastated at the prospect of losing his dynamic wife and fought bitterly to keep her, but lost out to the more manly English King. Eleanor was a fiercely independent lady, both mentally and financially, and led a long and adventurous life until she died at 82 in 1204.

Catherine de Medici, the widow of the French King Henri II, exercised profound power over her three sons, François II, Charles IX and Henri III, all of whom became Kings of France during her lifetime. Catherine was not a beauty, but has been called the most powerful woman of the 16th Century. It was this staunch Catholic who persuaded her son, King Charles IX, to carry out the wretched Saint

Bartholomew's Massacre in 1572, leaving hundreds of Protestants slaughtered in the streets of Paris. Her suffocating hold on her sons prompted rumors that she had become incestuous with one or more of her offspring after the tragic death of her husband. The formidable Catherine de Medici eventually drew a fifth king into her lair by arranging for her daughter, Margot, to marry Henry of Navarre, who ascended to the French throne in 1599 as King Henri IV.

Innumerable women in the past who were known for their genius in the creative arts won the favors of famous men in order to gain public recognition in the chauvinistic world of arts. Camille Claudel was able to sell her sculptures through the studio of her lover, Auguste Rodin. Juliette Drouet's writings were published by the editor of her paramour, Victor Hugo, and Louise Colet's career as a poet was furthered by her lovers Gustave Flaubert and Alfred de Vigny.

The strong-willed Aurore Dudevant was so determined to break into the male-oriented literary world that she changed her professional name to George Sand, often dressing in flamboyant men's clothing when she frequented clubs and bars with fellow writers. She was a woman who had many affairs with members of the same and of the opposite sex, including tempestuous relationships with Frederic Chopin and Alfred de Musset.

If seductiveness or charm didn't work, ambitious Frenchwomen found other methods to get things accomplished. The macabre "affair of the poisons" in 1679 scandalized the court of King Louis XIV. During

> "One hair of a woman draws more than a team of oxen."
>
> Proverb

"We always
long for
forbidden
things, and
desire what is
denied us."

Rabelais
(1483-1553)

the turbulent period when Madame de Maintenon
was edging Madame de Montespan out as favorite
mistress of the King, Montespan resorted to the love
potions of La Voisin, a known sorceress who lived
on the outskirts of Paris. The infamous Catherine
Montvoisin had a lucrative business of selling poisons,
fertility fetishes, and aphrodisiacs. She also performed
abortions using the discarded embryos in secret rituals and magic formulas. When the rumor leaked out
that someone from the inner circle of the King had
made several trips to La Voisin's notorious establishment, Louis XIV sent his guards to raid the evil
abode and close it down. He was shocked to learn
from the payment vouchers that many of his relatives
and members of the court were clients who had utilized the gruesome merchandise and services.

Resourceful or attractive ladies have continuously
managed to shape French history without being
overly puritanical about the tactics of their success.
Frenchwomen possess a pragmatic streak that allows
them to focus on the end result without wasting time
agonizing about the process. Undertaking treacherous means to acquire power seems to be acceptable
in France if decorum and refined manners are used
along the way. One rule Frenchwomen stand by is
the avoidance of forcing men to capitulate verbally
or physically in public, a tactic which seems to allow
Frenchmen to feel more secure about following a
female's orders in private.

For centuries Frenchwomen have found it advantageous to perfect their charms and wit in order to

quietly dominate men who stand in the forefront of political, financial and social circles. Because of the subtlety of their talents, women in France have been extremely successful in methods that are lucrative and fulfilling to their needs and desires, even though these actions are not easy to document. It is their well-established record of successes that has helped win Frenchwomen their world reputation as male-pleasers.

Flag-waving feminists are rare in France and, as a group, Frenchwomen would be hard put to argue the case that they are overpowered by males. For every story about exploitation of women in France there is a comparable tale of female opportunism. The French favor the term "resourceful" when referring to the women who control their country with a clandestine power whether that power is accomplished legally, intellectually, psychologically, or in the boudoir.

French females handle power skillfully while retaining a certain flirtatious femininity. This talent is the envy of women around the world. Other nationalities are mystified as they watch these adored Frenchwomen control their men with the firm hold of an iron hand in a velvet glove.

In the upcoming chapters we will probe the aura of elusive charm that surrounds the women of France. The subtleties of their coquetry and cleverness are not easy to mimic; however, certain lessons can be learned from Frenchwomen that will help bring more romance and adventure to any woman's life.

"Ideal love is put forth by poets."

Alphonse Daudet (1840-1897)

mistress or matrimony

"The chain of wedlock is so heavy that it takes two to carry it—sometimes three."

Alexandre Dumas (1802-1870)

It has been said that the two favorite sports in France are eating and adultery. The subject of mistresses and lovers, politely called the "extended family," does not evoke snickers or embarrassment in France—unless, of course, the legal wife or husband happens to be in the presence of the mate's lover.

The French are sophisticated and accepting when dealing with the variations that take place in emotional and physical configurations. Specialized counseling for sexual disorders barely exists in France, as the population generally considers matters of the flesh a creative area of personal choice and one of the more pleasant realities of life.

Keep in mind when viewing the French that their philosophies are intricately influenced by 1500 years of romantic and passionate traditions. And no matter how the rest of the world judges their actions, the French seem to be smugly satisfied with their cultural habits and idiosyncrasies.

Balancing basic survival needs with sensual gratification is a national pastime. The National Archives display hundreds of handsome parchment letters and official treaties that emphasize the importance the

Gauls place on satisfaction of the senses. The powerful nobles not only sealed their documents with deco-
rative seals for security, but further embellished the
message with elaborate silk cording and gold tassels
for the sake of beauty.

Stately 11th and 12th Century castles and for-
tresses were solidly built for safety from invaders; at
the same time, their magnificent stonework, friezes,
sculptures, carved wooden gates, and precious linen
flags appealed to the eye. Grandiose culinary skills
were developed to dazzle visually as well as to nour-
ish the body. Practicality alone does not satisfy the
complicated needs of the sensitive French soul.

The French multi-faceted taste patterns carry
over to the domestic scene as well. Until the 20th
Century, marriages in France were normally arranged
for monetary purposes and not based on physical
attraction. Passion was rarely a consideration
in ancient marriages of convenience. Most
marriage contracts were drawn up to facili-
tate the union of important assets and
land, or to join together an impressive
title with a desirable dowry.

Even though newlyweds were
encouraged to produce healthy heirs,
the marriage was not necessarily one
of satisfying sex. Thus, the embellish-
ment of a desirable mistress or lover
often was added to the marital picture.
Kings, queens, politicians, and all levels of
affluent society participated in the lively

practice of satisfying their carnal yearnings outside of the familial unit. French history is laced with the names of prominent illegitimate progeny and their descendants. Many of today's important family titles come from the "natural children" of King Louis XIV who were provided with advantageous titles and estates. The current Count Walenska and his family, who descend from Napoleon Bonaparte and his mistress, the Countess Walenska, still own the prestigious property in Paris that the egotistical Emperor willed to his "natural son." Scores of famous châteaux, such as Maintenon, Anet and Chenonceaux are closely associated with favorite mistresses of the royal court.

In his Conseils d'une Grandmère, Maupassant produces a dialogue between a grandmother born in the 18th Century and her idealistic granddaughter. It tells something of Gallic thought on the matter of marriage:

> "But, grandmère, marriage is sacred," said the girl. The old lady quivers, for her heart still belongs to the preceding age of gallantry, "Love is sacred," she replies, "but often, marriage and love have no connection. You get married to found a family and you found a family to constitute society. Society cannot do without marriage. If society is a chain, then every family is a link in that chain. When one gets married, one

"It is public scandal that gives offense; it is no sin to sin in secret."

Molière
(1622-1673)

is bound to respect a social code, common fortunes unite and work for the common interest, represented by wealth and children. One only gets married once, my dear, and that is because society demands it, but one may love twenty times, because nature has made us that way inclined. You see, marriage is a law, and love is an instinct that moves us to the right or to the left. Instincts are always strongest and it is wrong to resist them since they come from God, whereas laws are made by men."

Impressionable school age children are bombarded with similar French literature in their classes, along with colorful folklore about deadly duels and treacherous wars caused by jealousies among competitive husbands and lovers. Adultery has been so commonplace in the history of France that today it would be difficult to work up a major debate with the French on the topic of extramarital affairs as the subject is so integrated into their heritage, art, literature and politics.

A more important discussion relating to the topic of romantic adventures outside the conjugal contract, would be whether one had the good sense to use discretion in conducting the affair. Being discreet is a revered rule in France, and when combined with savoir faire and sangfroid, the French are considered world authorities on how to apply salve to almost any sticky situation.

Dignity, sensitivity, and courtesy are the unwritten requirements that apply to marital unions complicated by outside intimates. Wives, husbands, mistresses and lovers function together on a relatively peaceful basis in France when the players adhere to the non-verbal code of manners. Statistics of spousal homicide and physically abused mates register 40% lower in France than in the United States.

In the 12th Century, Count William IX of Aquitaine, the grandfather of Eleanor of Aquitaine, violated the etiquette required in courtly love. He wrote a song about "having bedded the wives of Lord Guarin, Lord Bernart and other nobles 188 times within a month." He was soundly chastised and given a fine for the indiscretions of exaggeration and boasting in public.

Less stringent rules apply in today's infidelity intrigues; however, old patterns of behavior are carried on in subtle ways among the contemporary French. It is considered proper for a husband and wife to operate as a family unit in the decisions concerning children, celebrations of major holidays, important public events and financial matters. A French wife who enjoys satisfying comforts, adoring children, public respect, or a fulfilling career of her own, very often chooses to be oblivious to a husband's harmless philandering. A workable family structure is meaningful in France and such partnerships are held together with stoic fortitude. In many cases if the wife is bored or if the mood strikes her, she may take a lover to balance the equation.

During a particularly somber period in her life when Madame d'Epinay first became aware of her

"Stolen pleasures are sweetest."

Proverb

husband's public appearance with his mistress, it was suggested to her by a close friend that taking a lover would be the best cure for wounded pride.

"No," she said, "I don't believe that a husband's wrongs authorize a woman to behave badly."

"What do you mean by behaving badly? I don't recommend for a moment that you should parade a lover or have him always around you. On the contrary, he should be the man who is seen in your company the least often. I would do away with obvious gifts, confidences and love letters. In a word all those trivialities that give slight satisfaction and expose one to a thousand troubles."

"Then you want me to have a lover with whom one never spends any time?"

"Not at all, but I don't want him to be seen often enough for people to wonder what to think," advised the friend.

"Ah, then you admit that in spite of so many precautions people will talk and my reputation will be lost."

"My poor child, everything upsets and frightens you. In this world let their tongues wag. Who is really interested enough to go out and verify all that is said? How scintillating is a woman who is never talked about? The important thing is the choice in a lover and the use of discretion. People will talk about it for eight days and then they won't think anymore about you except to approve your actions."

Some wives have little interest in exerting the energy it takes to carry on with a lover even though their husband has a mistress. When the literary giant of the 19th Century, Victor Hugo, was on a long vacation with Juliette Drouet, his adored mistress, his wife, Adele, fully aware of her husband's companion, wrote him in July 1835.

"Do not deny yourself anything. I have no more need of pleasures of the body, it is calm I need. I am quite old in my tastes—what better is there left for me in this life? I have only one desire, and it is that those I love should be happy. Never shall I abuse my rights which marriage has given me over you, my poor friend, you who married at twenty. I do not wish to bind your life to the old woman I have become. Thus, at least, whatever you give me you will give me freely, and in all liberty. Do not trouble yourself about it. I embrace you. Be happy, very happy."

Adele Hugo, with much dignity, continued as "queen" of Victor Hugo's large household, remaining at the head of his table, devoting herself to her growing children, watching over the family's properties. Outwardly nothing had changed when Hugo's mistress came into his life, and a lack of change was what he wanted. Meanwhile, he assured Adele that he "would always love her, though differently."

The guidelines are still fairly well-defined within the French domestic hierarchy. Due to the high expense involved, today's French families tend to be smaller, but children are adored and their welfare is tenderly shared by both parents. Proper upbringing and education is of prime concern, and decorum calls for appropriate living conditions and expenses of the

family to take precedence over excessive luxuries for a mistress.

When business or social functions call for the distinguished presence of the wife, a generous allowance is provided for her wardrobe and a dignified display of jewels for her to demonstrate her superior position.

A savvy French mistress who has managed to make herself comfortable and well-provided for does not create unreasonable demands, nor does she allow a detectable greediness to become a problem. She cleverly remains agreeable about sharing time and budgets with the lawful family members and in return is usually rewarded for her patience and understanding.

Although it is considered foolish for experienced mistresses to become naggers, there are times when she can despair in her loneliness without the man she adores, especially during the traditional holidays that he is expected to spend with his family. If the sentimental weeping takes on just the right tone, it is likely suitable gifts will appear to assuage the pain of the lonesome mistress.

Confrontation between the wife and "the other woman" should be avoided if at all possible. Nothing good can come of a meeting between two women who feel as if they alone occupy the stellar position in one man's existence.

Discretion is key. Even though the physical condition and habits of the wife may be a great curiosity to the paramour of the husband, she must resist the urge to travel in the same circles. It is up to the mistress to stay clear of the wife's hairdresser, tennis club, place of work, boulangerie and dressmaker. She has probably heard more than she cares to about her lover's mate and therefore is aware of the schedules and social patterns to avoid.

Opening nights of the social season can be attended by both wife and mistress, but seating should be at a safe distance in private boxes at the opera or ballet so an adroit gentleman can share his company discreetly between the two during intermissions.

Mutual friends should be diplomatic and avoid the temptation of instigating an electrifying encounter of husband and mistress for the mere sake of excitement. It isn't a nice thing to do and the drama can have an unhappy ending.

If the unfortunate meeting between the two women does occur, hopefully it is not at a seated dinner party, because the atmosphere could become volatile. If a woman wants to keep a married man as her lover, she should realize that men who are involved in the balancing act of business, family, and mistress do not welcome pointless agitation.

If an unfortunate encounter does take place between a wife and a mistress, the contact should be as brief as possible. Neither party should tax themselves to come up with a clever quip; the situation is clearly too awkward to be of any value. Make the chance meeting bland and benign so it can fade away with a quick exit. Rarely is a ménage à trois gracefully compatible, so don't buck the odds.

The chances that a European man will divorce his wife of long standing and marry a mistress are remote. Even though only 14% of the French attend mass on a regular basis, France is traditionally a Catholic country and there are plenty of saints, cathedrals, and crucifixes around as constant reminders that divorce is not an easy option to pull off in view of the national religion.

Divorce in France is an expensive and complicated procedure, and thus a mistress is unlikely to wish for such an event. French law courts are sluggish and there are few winners financially, as property usually stays within original family boundaries. Status quo is the preferred choice for most Frenchmen, as it is more acceptable in French business and social circles to have a bizarre marital arrangement than to have a well-organized divorce.

Men prefer the routine of their normal habits rather than taking the time and effort required for a legal dissolution that will give them few advantages. It is more agreeable for them to stay in the good graces of their beloved children and keep up public appearances while leaving the marriage contract undisturbed. In most cases, Frenchmen have figured out how to compensate a mistress physically, financially and emotionally so she will go along with the scheme. On the other hand, French women are duly tolerant when the situation suits them.

Glamorous mistresses can be expensive and few men can afford the luxury; however, there are still powerful politicians and international magnates who can indulge in the age old practice. There are many independent-minded French career women today who do not necessarily insist on being kept in grand style in order to carry on with a married man.

Quality companionship is harder to come by these days, and personal needs are being fulfilled on a less demanding basis. Physical satisfaction, candlelight dinners, adoring compliments, and sentimental gifts can be sufficient gratification to many modern professional women who have little trouble supporting themselves and no problems with guilt. Self-pity and guilt are not big factors in the proud French psyche.

Stoically, French wives manage to appear dignified when they are aware that they are married to a womanizer—that is, if their lifestyle is not overly impinged upon. Likewise, when a recognized mistress accompanies a man who has a separate family life, there are no explanations made nor asked for by the surrounding company.

Friends and associates pay little heed to the details of one another's intimate lives, unless a gross flaunting of indiscretion is evident. The French are tolerant of each others' private habits and sexual preferences if the all-important good manners are observed.

Romance is an essential part of the French way of life. The French are surrounded from birth by sensuous statues, adventurous folklore, romantic art, and endless national relics saluting valor for the sake of love. Frenchmen still like to think of themselves as possessing the characteristics of chivalry: courage, courtesy, generosity, loyalty, and honor. French women as well as American women find the old world traditions of a continental gentleman fascinating, and can still be charmed by having their hand brushed lightly with a kiss.

The women in France are keenly skilled in the art of nurturing this exalted attitude of chivalrous manners. Wives demand respect and mistresses expect generosity and loyalty. Long term mistresses manage to relay the message that they have gladly given up the opportunity for a suitable marriage in order to share the sublime company of a beloved man. Hearing just the right tone of unselfishness in a beloved lady's voice can bring out the generous side of even the most frugal man.

An ambitious mistress aspires to gather valuable real estate, jewels and other assets in her name in the event something dreadful should happen to her protector. Acts of thoughtful benevolence by a lover can help a mistress feel secure about her future even though he is not there to personally help her. Generous gifts during his lifetime can avoid the embarrassment of naming "an outside female" in his will.

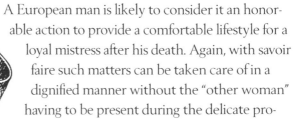

A European man is likely to consider it an honorable action to provide a comfortable lifestyle for a loyal mistress after his death. Again, with savoir faire such matters can be taken care of in a dignified manner without the "other woman" having to be present during the delicate proceedings of the probate hearing. A suave Frenchman can rest in peace with his manly reputation left intact when he has taken care of the needs of his family and arranged for his mistress to have income property in her own name.

When the cast of characters in a Frenchman's domestic and romantic scenario are all satisfied with their lot, life and death can go on in a civilized manner in this country that insists on enjoying creativity, style, and sensations of the heart and soul above all else.

putting your best leg forward

"The most beautiful make-up on a woman is passion. But cosmetics are easier to buy."

Yves Saint-Laurent
(1936-)

France is a nation known to hold visual aesthetics in high regard; in fact, the idea of beauty is as important to the French as the air they breathe. Their architecture, parks, bridges, market displays, clothing, cuisine and personal style all reflect the high priority they place on balance, form, and color. They take particular delight when all these natural and creative enhancements involve attractive women, and this preoccupation with the female gender shows up everywhere in their sensuous way of living for love.

"A court without women is like a spring without flowers," proclaimed the gallant King François I in 1515. During the reign of this brilliant and cultivated man there was a rediscovery of classical antiquity with its cult of beauty and intellect. François I became acutely aware of the treasures that were being produced by the Italian Renaissance and lost no time in seeking out talented Italian artisans willing to travel to France with their tools and skills ready to embellish his palaces. He was determined to duplicate the lush style that was proliferating in Florence under

"All styles are good except the tiresome sort."

Voltaire
(1694-1778)

the Medicis, and he joyfully took part in the planning by encouraging his new artistic team to exalt the female form in statuary, paintings, books, and theatre.

In fact, King François I admired Leonardo di Vinci to such an extent that he offered the Florentine genius a comfortable château near the royal palace in the Loire Valley to live and work for the rest of his life. Being under intense criticism in Italy at the time, Leonardo accepted the flattering offer leaving Florence with his painting of the Mona Lisa under his arm. The French king was desolate when di Vinci died in 1519 only four years after becoming a revered member of the French royal court.

"Beauty is but the splendor of God and divine light extended to all created objects, but the divine reflection has chosen to shine with the greatest brilliance in woman's body," wrote the 16th Century French philosopher, Agrippa , in his Excellence of Women. Is it any wonder that French women have acquired confidence in their sexuality after centuries of constant praise and worship? Dating from early in French history, beautiful women have been kept on a lofty pedestal, and they have grown even more attractive and sophisticated under the continued nurturing of praise for their talents.

In the Middle Ages females began to focus more on artistic clothing and jewelry, but even then it was considered important to possess a high forehead proving that one had brains as well as beauty. Many women of the era shaved their hairline back giving the effect of a well-developed brain within a dramatically shaped head. The popularity of the "beauty and brains" combination continues to be important to today's Frenchwomen who cleverly incorporate intelligence, wit, and thoughtful seduction to enhance their physical charms.

If one wants to delve into specific beauty secrets dating as far back as the 9th Century, the Bibliothèque nationale de France is brimming with tomes detailing the treatment, adornment and care of a woman's body. There are hundreds of volumes detailing every aspect of female attractiveness and charm. The 16th Century writer on hygiene, Marie de Romieu, advises members of her sex to bathe "as least once within the month to keep themselves clean for their own comfort and for the pleasure of their husbands." She also suggests that "sponges soaked in rosewater should be placed under their armpits and between their thighs while making certain that one's undergarments be kept fresh and dainty," (an uncommon habit in the Middle Ages due to scanty supplies of soap and heated water).

Diane de Poitiers, King Henri II's mistress, was the great beauty ideal of the 1500s. She was among the stunning noble ladies who were gathered around Henri's father to illuminate the colorful celebrations and festivals held for the pleasure of the royal entourage. When Henri was only twelve years old, he immediately became attracted to Diane who was seated next to his father, King François I, at a jousting tournament. The young heir to the throne brazenly bowed to Diane with boyish infatuation even

"Ideal beauty
is a fugitive
which is never
located."

Madame de
Sévigné

(1626-1696)

though she was twenty years older than he and was then married to the Comte de Maulevrier. Only a few years after that first encounter Diane de Poitiers succumbed to the charms of the young prince and thereafter forever remained the love of his life. When Henri became King he was obliged to take the Italian Catherine de Medici for his official wife and dutifully sired eight children; however, the lovely Diane held the key to Henri's heart until his accidental death in 1559.

Diane's beauty secrets were the talk of the kingdom during the 16th Century, and she remains a glamourous legend in France to this day. Her contemporaries accused her of participating in occult formulas and secret potions, but in spite of the sometimes malicious gossip, everyone found her ravishing. Diane was the fashion leader of the era and the grande dames of the upper classes copied her manners, her hair styles, and her way of dressing. The most famous artists of the Renaissance used Diane as the idealized model for their portraits and sculptures, many of which can be seen today in the Louvre and other prestigious museums.

This famous seductress was a strong, statuesque and sportive type with refined features; and although her beauty regime is well documented, it is not an easy one to duplicate. Diane arose before six every morning and took a full body bath in icy water, convinced that the cold immersions safeguarded her radiant complexion and her enviable energy. She began a whole new trend for bathing in preserved rain water daily and soaking in asses' milk at least once a week. No matter what the weather, Diane insisted on regular exercise and went horseback riding in the fresh air of the royal forests each morning. In the evenings King Henri ordered gargantuan feasts for his court; however, Diane was prone to be a vegetarian and ordered mostly fruits, nuts and fresh produce from her own servants when eating at the King's table.

Since early childhood, the privileged young Diane was gifted with smooth white skin, robust health, and high firm breasts. She was a precocious child and became an accomplished horsewoman by the time she was six years old, riding her favorite stallion for hours each day while acting out her mythological name, Diane, Goddess of the Hunt. From the beginning everything was in place to carry her to her destiny as the female idol of the times.

The Queen knew of Henri's obsession with his mistress from the onset of the royal marriage and Catherine was tortured by jealousy, constantly trying to discover the bewitching love techniques used by this rival. The Queen went so far as to have holes drilled in the ceiling above Diane's apartment in the Palace in order to spy on her husband's meetings with his mistress.

Brantôme, the court gossip and chronicler wrote, "The queen spied on a very lovely, white, delicate and fresh woman, who was half-naked, clad in a chemise, caressing her lover with a flourish of feathers, charm

"A well turned-out woman is never ugly."

Proverb

and delicious folly, which her lover returned until they slid from the bed onto the floor and still in their chemises, pursued their acrobatics on the plush carpet, so avoiding the heat of the bed, for it was in the middle of a warm summer day."

A few years after Henri's untimely death, Brantôme went to visit Diane when she became ill after being exiled to her château in Normandy. He wrote that "she was still beautiful at sixty-five and had not resorted to any beauty artifices, except that she continued to drink a broth of alchemist's drugs every morning." When she died he lamented in his diary, "What a pity that earth should have to be heaped over such a gorgeous body."

Of course ideas about beauty standards change through time, and by the 18th Century the feminine form was rounder, noses straighter, faces fuller and make-up more dramatic. Wardrobes and grooming habits took on the lushness and frenzy of Louis XIV's lifestyle at Versailles which eventually blossomed into a full-blown Romanticism affecting all the arts. Under the focus of so much attention women put more and more emphasis on their physical appearance. They were also better educated and confident in their power to civilize their men—or corrupt them, as the case may have been.

Frenchmen have long adored dramatic spectacles of all types, especially those involving women, and they have lavished their ladies with exotic jewels, fabulous wardrobes, flattery and idolization. With these welcomed rewards, Frenchwomen have developed a sharp competitive spirit to vie for the biggest prizes such as the power that comes with being the mistress of a high official, fame as the subject of illustrious works of art, or great wealth in appreciation of their feminine attributes. There is also the bonus of pride and satisfaction in knowing that one is admired and sought after by great men. It is easier to fathom the excessive importance that the French place on style and beauty and the obsession seems more rational when one considers the benefits that have been lavished upon the beauty goddesses of the past.

Foreigners who continue to be baffled by the inexplicable sexiness surrounding Parisian women must stop to realize that this particular allure has been hundreds of years of inspiration in the making. The French aura of femininity is tough to decipher because it is so intricately tied in with innate Gallic characteristics and upbringing; however, the more obvious tactics of seductiveness can be brought into focus if one is curious enough to pursue the fascinating formula.

The healthy level of self-assurance that most Frenchwomen possess plays a major role in their ability to acquire power and to use it successfully. Being confident and comfortable with oneself is infinitely more difficult than it sounds, especially if one has not grown up in an atmosphere of praise and flattery nor has had the advantage of a French mother who emphasizes wise boudoir secrets and clever beauty techniques. Even though they may have been brought up in meager homes, adolescents in France are likely to be exposed to sophisticated aesthetics and chivalry due to the rich offerings of the public arts programs, the colorful action in the cafés and parks, and the emphasis on national pride in the energetic school curriculum.

Napoleon Bonaparte, who was a great admirer of women, said "a woman needs to spend six months in Paris before she can begin to realize the extent of her power. The women here are the most captivating in the world and they soon learn to become la grande affaire (the main event)."

Parisian women have the reputation of possessing a natural flare for fashion; however, I'm not convinced that the enviable look they exude is as guileless and unplanned as it appears. After probing into the agendas of contemporary Parisians, I see indications of heroic efforts in beauty rituals such as regular facials, hair coloring, waxing, peeling, weekly massages, "taking the waters," shopping the couture sales, and studying expert advice on current makeup tips. They quietly involve themselves in caring for their body in order to present an appearance of unadorned glowing health rather than of hiding behind a mask of cosmetics.

Treatment and care of their skin has always been more important to Frenchwomen than merely camouflaging their problems with make up. Today's leading cosmetic companies sell a ratio of 65% treatment products to 35% makeup items in France in contrast to sales in the United States that are primarily concealers, powder and color products versus fewer items in the treatment lines.

"Taking the waters" at one of the many mineral springs is a common practice among the French. The well-known natural springs at Vittel, Evian, Vichy or the saltwater thalasso treatment centers on the North Atlantic coast are busy year round with European men and women flushing the toxins out of their systems with therapeutic water regimes. Many of these health and beauty habits have been going on for thousands of years as shown by the evidence of archaeological ruins which exist on the premises of today's thriving thermal spas.

The benefits of therapeutic water treatments are not limited to the affluent in France, as all income groups have a choice of popularly priced rates to choose from. In fact, many of the "cure" programs are prescribed by doctors and covered by the national medical benefits. Following a week's agenda of invigorating salt water rubs and algae wraps, one's skin is left glowing and can appear radiant with minimal makeup. These popular water rituals are considered a key ingredient to the natural vitality and youthfulness that Frenchwomen maintain in their advanced years.

Obesity is rare in France, at least up to the present time. The nation is known for its inspired cuisine and even average income families seldom eat fast or frozen foods. The French prefer to rely on daily shopping trips to select their fresh vegetables, fruits, fish, eggs and tasty cheeses, leaving red meat for special occasions. The main meals are still a family event and the congenial ambiance of the gathering along with

"Good clothes open all doors."

Proverb

"Fine feathers
make fine
friends."

Proverh

red wine and expert preparation seems to keep their digestive systems in balance. One sees little consumption of food while a person is on the run, except for the traditional pain au chocolat as an after school treat.

Menus are usually nourishing and satisfying, a fact that eliminates the need for constant snacks and soft drinks. The French adore the movies, but popcorn is not part of the scene, and they do not sit for hours in front of the television with peanuts and potato chips at their side. The French are more involved with physical entertainments such as taking walks in the parks and countryside, bicycling, and lovemaking; thus, they stay in form without all the scheduled gym classes and personal trainers that are popular in the United States. Basically the French use common sense about eating and exercise without over emphasizing the subject of diets, especially in mixed company.

The most obvious flaw in this exemplary picture of body care is the high consumption of cigarettes. At last, however, the anti-smoking campaign has caught hold in France, and there are fewer fumes in the local brasseries and restaurants, but be prepared for plenty of puffers in the older bars and ancient cafés.

Along with looking physically in shape and naturally healthy, Frenchwomen relay the illusive charm of "accidental allure" which mystifies visiting Americans. One wonders how the average Parisian can walk down the street looking so haphazard and unconcerned about fashion and yet appear so provocative.

Sometimes called "seductive disarray," a sensuous
lady can give the provocative impression that she just
rolled out of someone's bed and is sauntering home
in the middle of the afternoon.

Men seem to like this "devil may care" nonchalance, especially businessmen who are obliged to
keep everything well-organized at the office. It signals
to them a wild, careless and dangerous women, a real
handful of surprises. They either want to tame her or
get in on the action. Many tend to agree that women
can appear sexier when things go a little haywire with
their appearance. It sends a message of vulnerability
and helplessness. There's a tarty look to smeared lipstick, and chipped fingernails, signaling that "this girl
is living on the wild side and is probably not uptight
about her love life."

When Frenchwomen do decide to pull it together
for a special occasion, they manage to create an individual style groomed with creative sophistication,
but without an impression of calculated perfection.
Although spectacular hairdos can be seen at gala balls
in France, the ladies also know how to let their hair
down and allow their curls to blow with the breeze.
Simple bangs and shoulder length hair is one of the
youthful looks that Parisian women like to swing
with until well into their eighties. They are aware
that having a hairdo sprayed in place can throw out a
cautionary barrier to men who are intimidated about
approaching such an organized creature.

Again, it comes down to the French attitude of
being comfortable and secure about one's own body

> "There is only
> one proper
> way to wear a
> beautiful dress:
> to forget you
> are wearing it."
>
> Madame de
> Girardin

while going along with what life has to offer. This relaxed feeling about being natural relays the idea that French girls are more approachable and open to nature's instincts.

Being well-groomed has a different meaning to Frenchwomen than it does to most American women. The French have mastered a "looseness of style" in the final stage of readiness that manages to stop short of appearing contrived. For the right occasion a severe, lacquered hairdo may produce a dramatic theatrical effect; however, the coquette will use the charm of seductive disarray when she's on the prowl for conquests.

Frenchwomen are famous for their frugality, yet they are masterful at looking like a million on a small allowance. With only a few quality couture pieces, they have the knack to build an impressive wardrobe by using their creative skills. From the time French girls first learn to walk they are exposed to the bou-

tique windows of great designers and these visual lessons have tuned their eyes to a keen perception of balance and color. By the time they are into their teens, they know how to tie a scarf, wear jewelry properly, put a saucy bow in their hair, and cinch in their waist with a wide belt. They usually buy clothes that show off the figure and are able to complete a simple ensemble by adding spice with a piece of antique lace or a feather boa around their neck. They grow up learning how to flirt with their eyes as well as with their evocative clothing.

The French nature is too independent to be content with a coordinated outfit as it comes off the rack. On the streets of Paris, one can see a $3000 Chanel jacket flung over a simple white Hanes tee shirt and tight jeans, or a skimpy black skirt with a luxurious antique lace blouse. In general, Frenchwomen feel secure following individual instincts without worrying about what others are wearing or thinking. The mere fact that they know they have a world reputation for being chic gives them the courage to experiment with their own ideas about fashion.

What appears to come naturally to the French may take more effort for the rest of the world to accomplish, but the "sense of self" that is imperative to the French mystique is a good start and is available to almost everyone who is willing to work for it.

an invitation into the private chamber

"An open door
may tempt
a saint."

Proverb

When a suitor is at last honored with an invitation to the private chambers of a French lady, more than likely an intoxicating experience awaits him. Upon stepping into the cozy confines of an enlightened coquette, one can quickly see that an interior decorator has not set foot in the place, as it is far too personal for any signature other than the owner's.

While the services of decorators in France are commonly called upon for hotels, restaurants and boutiques, those of true French character most often choose to arrange their own dwellings in an idiosyncratic manner with personal souvenirs, collectibles, heirlooms and arty pieces that suit themselves. The unique charm of French individuality carries throughout every aspect of their lives, as expressed in their dress, diets, conversations, opinions and the originality of their private domains.

It is difficult to generalize when describing a Parisian residence, except in the case of historic 17th and 18th Century salons that have been carefully restored by the state and opened as public monuments. The formal salons of that era accommodated the stilted manners demanded by the courts of Louis XIV and Louis XV and frequently strict rules applied to the evening agendas of dining, card games, conversation, and music. Warmth was breathed into

"Men have sight; women insight."

Victor Hugo
(1802-1885)

the formal gilded surroundings by the eccentric courtesans, grande dames, and members of the royal family who held sway as hostesses in these posh quarters. It was not until after the Revolution of 1789 that proper women were allowed to be seen in public eating establishments. Even then, it was considered adventurous for a lady of the upper class to eat in a restaurant other than at a stagecoach stopover.

One's home is sacred to the French and privacy is a guarded luxury. If an invitation to their private quarters is extended, it is meant as a compliment and a sign that you are considered one of their inner circle of friends. If, in fact, you are invited as the solitary guest for an intimate dinner cooked by the hostess, be prepared for romance. Take flowers or champagne, chocolates and your toothbrush.

Before accepting such a highly prized invitation, try to weigh your intentions toward the lady or gentleman hosting the tête-à-tête because once you have crossed the threshold of the inner sanctum and are drinking good wine in the dim atmosphere of candlelight and exotic scents, your judgment will be no longer be reliable.

Today, many Parisian apartments are small due to the exorbitant cost of real estate in the capital city, so careful use of each available square meter is paramount. There are still magnificent spaces of grand proportions that exist, usually legacies from past eras now tightly controlled by a committee of descendants, but the heirs of these large 18th and 19th Century apartments are often forced to divide up the properties to rent in order to contend with the costly maintenance and the heavy inheritance taxes.

Enterprising Parisians, however, are adroit at making whatever space they dwell in work in their favor. They possess the savvy to transform small into cozy or minuscule into intimate. When a guest falls under the spell of fine champagne served in antique crystal with flickering candlelight, he begins to believe that the hostess could afford any haven she desires, but prefers this precious cocoon for its tender proportions.

Gracious old French households consist of a fascinating conglomeration of various threadbare rugs over creaky parquet floors, richly framed paintings by unknown artists, yellowed sketches of provocative boudoir scenes, faded velvet shadow boxes displaying old opera glasses and lace fans, cushy loveseats, fringed satin curtains, chipped Baccarat chandeliers, dusty leather bound books, languid ferns, ancient non-ticking clocks, exquisite porcelain serving pieces, dented sterling, and tapestry pillows, combined with the most wondrous collection of period furniture from various ancestors. Miraculously, this menagerie can fall together with surprising effectiveness and personal style. Almost always one can detect the element of whimsy present in a household where a true Frank has hibernated for a number of years.

There is no doubt in the mind of a privileged visitor that he is behind the scenes of something decidedly personal, maybe even privy to guarded family treasures, and that he has been accepted as a

> "The whole pleasure in love lies in the variety."
>
> Molière.
> (1622-1673)

trusted confident. Already his ego has been bolstered
with the honor of access upon the hallowed ground.
The indulgent hostess continues to lead the invitee
through an alluring and delightful scenario which
could easily end up in the final act behind the velvet
curtain.

It all starts with the grand welcome. The flattering acknowledgement at the door of a French home
surpasses any greeting given in public. An invisible
red carpet is rolled out as if the door has been opened
to find a "prince of the royal blood." The reception
of guests is a studied art in Europe and the event is
considered a significant factor by the Michelin Guide
when dispensing its coveted three-star ratings to restaurants.

More than likely the rooms will be bathed in dim
lighting and candles, hiding the cracks in the ceiling
and softening any lines on the brow of the lady. Floral
fragrances will waft from fresh cut flowers, and exotic
herbal aromas will glide in from the kitchen. Mozart,
Debussy or Charles Aznavour's ballads are lingering
in the corners with nary a television in sight. The
honored guest is given the impression that the staff
has just been excused through the servants' door leaving the evening for uninterrupted pleasures. The willing guest is magnetically drawn into the spider's lair
farther and farther removed from the harsh outside
world he has left behind.

The ambiance has been set like a stage, with star
billing going to the guest while the presiding hostess
expertly excels in her supporting role. The artfulness

of the situation is in the subtlety of knowing how
heavy to cast the spell, not layering it on too thick,
but providing all the right ingredients for seduction.
It is unusual for a man to feel overly pampered or
adored; however, it is up to the sensitivity of the mistress of the manor to gauge the appropriate degree of
intimacy without putting the "target" on his guard.
Frenchwomen are masters at giving playful signals
which leave just enough question about the outcome
for a man to exercise his inherent need for the chase
and final capture.

A small scale dining table, draped to the floor with
a random piece of rich brocade, is set for two with a
comfortable armchair only an arm's reach from the
position of the hostess. The delightful table glistens
with crystal and unmatched heirloom silver (the
French are not obsessed with owning matched sets,
quality counts more). A towering candelabra flickers
in the center, high enough to assure that facial features are not, heaven forbid, lighted from below
the chin thus accentuating gravity damage. If
the luxury of a fireplace exists, without fail it
will be glowing and emitting sensations of security and warmth.

When the tender scene progresses with
mounting success and the menu (more about
captivating cuisine in another chapter) has been
light enough to encourage after-dinner parlor
games rather than a snooze, then it's natural
that things will grow toward a more intimate
level.

Going from dining room to bed chamber should include enough anticipatory pauses to tease the senses and feed the flames. The hostess will suggest an interlude on the feather-filled settee in front of the fireplace with scores of candles and soft music to mellow the mood for Cognac and chocolate kisses. French females perform glowingly at this point. Overall they are superb at intimate conversation that becomes provocative while supposedly discussing cerebral matters such as philosophy, literature, or history. It doesn't take long for a debate about famous writers or politicians to land upon a poignant love scandal involving irresistible attraction, the clandestine chase and the power of forbidden passion.

At this point a French damsel may quote Bernard of Ventador, the 12th Century troubadour, who wrote, "By nothing is man made so worthy as by love and the courtship of women." Such a lofty thought to identify with and perhaps to test one's own worthiness.

Motives for lovemaking suddenly seem lifted from animalistic instincts to a level of intellectual greatness, following the same pursuits of the passion-driven geniuses like King Henri IV, Molière, Châteaubriand, Napoleon, Victor Hugo, Franz Liszt and hundreds of other sexually ardent heroes.

Boudoirs and bed chambers have long been favorite meeting venues for French intellectuals. In the wintertime, King Louis XIV received his admirers while sitting in fur robes and propped up in his luxurious, canopied bed. He was warm and comfortable there during the long sessions of listening to his councilors while duly impressing them with the richness of his scrumptiously decorated sleeping quarters.

After Louis XIV died in 1715, rooms became smaller and furniture was adapted to the more intimate proportions. Curtained beds gave way to cozy alcoves, and embroidered silk covered the walls. Matching divans and chaise lounges tufted in satin and fringe were positioned in comfortable groupings to encourage private conversations. Women received their callers while they made up at their dressing tables or drank their morning coffee in front of a dainty fireplace. Sofas and chairs were custom made in every conceivable shape and size destined for all types of intimate activities often given names like the gondola, the conversational, the confident, and the tête-à-tête.

Society ladies entertained guests of both sexes in their baths after bathing became more fashionable with the advent of prestigious indoor plumbing in the palaces and elegant homes. Some stylish ladies had adjustable wooden lids made to slip over their bath water whenever they received visitors, while others merely whitened the water with bubbles or milk of almonds.

Luxury boudoirs of the 18th Century were provided with the hygienic fixture which Anglo-Saxons had been too prudish to adopt—the bidet. The first bidets were works of art enclosed in magnificent cases made of hand-tooled leather or carved wood. Of course for mistresses of the King, the bidet was of prime importance and Madame de Pompadour possessed one

"To scare a bird is not the way to catch it."

Proverb

"There is a
woman at the
beginning of all
things great."

Alphonse de
Lamartine

(1790-1869)

with gilded feet and a crested rosewood lid.

While staying at the Château de Cirey near Paris, Madame de Graffigny wrote a letter dated December 4, 1738, describing the boudoir of her hostess, Madame du Châtelet, who was Voltaire's mistress: "Her bedroom is paneled in yellow and pale blue, the alcove is lined with India wallpaper, the bed is covered in blue silk moiré. Everything matches, even the dog's basket and pillow. The whole chamber is so pretty, one could fall to one's knees in adoration. Each panel has a painting by Watteau, the ceiling is being done by a pupil of his who has been working at Cirey for three years. Such jewels and snuffboxes, 15 or 20 of them in gold and lacquer and precious stones! And then the bathroom, sheer enchantment! All tile except for a marble floor and porcelain baths. The little cabine de toilette is paneled in green lacquered wood - gay, gilded and divinely carved - with a little sofa and chair in the same carved wood."

Madame du Châtelet's daily bathing schedule was legendary at the time when bathing could be put off for weeks due to the cold interiors of the country châteaux. While dressed in frilly lounging apparel, this intellectual lady had readings and cozy gatherings for Voltaire in her private bed chamber until the early hours of the morning.

After peeking into a few bedrooms of today's grande dames, one becomes less mystified as to the success of the seemingly over-abundance of fancy bed and bath boutiques throughout France. If a Parisian hostess has premeditated notions of serving up the paramount dessert, you can be certain that the bed-chamber will be prepared accordingly, in other words, "fit for a feast."

The extravagance of owning the world's finest silk-like cotton Porthault sheets and pillow shams is considered a worthwhile investment among savvy European seductresses. Men do not often purchase lacy white bed linens nor indulge in outrageously priced embroidered duvets, comforters and blanket covers, but it is rare that they can resist sinking into these luxurious linens without a sensation of joy.

A billowing white virginal bed with clouds of goosedown tasseled pillows smelling of sentimental lavender lifts a man's thoughts to heavenly heights. Perhaps the contrast of such feminine finery com-pared to their own sleeping quarters is part of the captivating fascination that grips most men as they are enveloped in the sensuous folds of softness.

Supplying a home with sheets, pillowcases, towels and tableware in the United States is often treated as a chore of necessity. Damsels in France dress their beds with the same care and consideration that they give to their selection of underwear. They place great importance on the art of visual coquetry, thus setting up an atmosphere to best frame all their other prac-ticed flirtations. The extra effort is not considered an imposition, but an opportunity to participate in the agreeable art of allure. "A bed is love's theatre," said Honoré de Balzac in 1830.

Madame Recamier was a trendsetter in 19th Century interior design with her exquisite taste and her love of Greek antiquities and Egyptian motifs which were inspired by Napoleon's ambitious campaigns to Egypt. Her bed was truly a stage setting. It was painted antique white with gold-leaf trim, placed as a high altar upon a raised platform and half hidden by sheer muslin curtains hanging from a garland of bronze flowers. Upon one of the steps leading up to the bed was a dark genie on a white marble base holding a golden bronze lamp guiding the way to paradise.

Elegant and intimate attention to detail can be enchantingly relayed in a 500-square-foot pied-à-terre or graciously achieved in a grandiose townhouse. The secret is the skillful knack of assembling unexpected and sentimental minutia, an art that Frenchwomen have mastered, even when they are hampered by

spartan budgets or cramped spaces. Outsiders are often baffled when they try to duplicate the whimsical quality in French decor and dress, which may appear to the untrained eye as haphazardly thrown together. Don't be fooled. There is nothing nonchalant about this seductive lair; it is intentionally thought-out and reflects a practiced art of allure.

I've reluctantly come to believe that the ability to perform such magic with odds and ends is an inbred talent with the

French and that the ability has a great deal to do with their refined memory genes. I'm not ready to give up the challenge, however, and feel that we Anglos, with practice, exposure, and keen determination, can somehow acquire some of the skills of wondrous seductiveness that hovers around the image of the femme fatale.

french perfume that rocks the room

"Perfumes are the greatest traitors in the world; they herald, they outline, and they declare the most delicious of intentions."

Paul Valéry
(1871-1945)

Documented evidence exists that perfumed oils were exquisitely bottled in Egypt during Cleopatra's lifetime. Pressed citrus and floral essences were also used in the bath houses frequented by the wealthy citizens of early Roman times. Yet the French have no qualms about claiming credit for the creation of perfume only 500 years ago for the sophisticated court of King François I.

Like bubbly champagne, which may be imitated by wine growers around the world but must come from the French region of Champagne to have true status, perfume carrying the ultimate mark of distinction must be produced in France. The universal reputation of French perfume is one more ingenious marketing story the French have managed to sell to a world hungry for glamour and romance.

Always creative and resourceful at touting their own talents, whether their accomplishments are valid or exaggerated, French entrepreneurs deserve respect for successfully proclaiming themselves supreme authorities in the domain of allure and seduction.

The actual reasons why the sweet smelling extracts came into vogue with aristocrats of the 16th Century did not have a particularly glamorous basis.

The beautifully decorated, but unventilated, salons were packed on gala evenings with frolicking French socialites who bathed infrequently. Moreover, during the colder months affluent people wore layers of woolen garments topped by silks and satins which looked elegant but did not have the benefit of modern-day dry cleaning. When it was too damp and icy to open the windows for fresh air, party guests were very happy, for obvious reasons, to catch a whiff of flowers or spices surrounding a pretty lady.

Women wore tiny bunches of violets or tuberoses tucked in their bosom during social events, and among the privileged set it became the rage to dab distilled oils of rose petals or orange blossoms on strategic parts of the body for romantic occasions. It was expected that fresh floral bouquets from indoor hothouses would freshen the household atmosphere of all the noble mansions and royal palaces.

The demand for seductive aromas quickly gained popularity with all those who could afford the costly extravagance. Very chic ladies wore leather gloves impregnated with musk, lavender, or rose oil and  then added finger rings with tiny hinged boxes holding a few grains of aromatic spices. Dried rose petals were placed in dainty silk bags and then conveniently tucked into corsets and pantaloons of women who wished to enhance their sex appeal.

The most prestigious estates had "still-rooms" in which the guarded family recipes for perfumes and domestic medicines were prepared. Ladies of rank took great pride in their hand-written notebooks of secret elixirs, and the valuable formulas were carefully handed down from one generation to another.

The civilized ritual of tub baths came into fashion in the 18th Century after effective room heaters made the drafty châteaux more comfortable. Voltaire considered bathing in rose water or jasmine lotions the "luxury of luxuries," and he asserted that it was wrong to believe the gossip of the day that "only women of easy virtue were in the habit of bathing daily in fragrant waters."

After centuries of study and interest in the arts of making themselves more attractive by using artificial aids, applications and perfumes, Frenchwomen have become highly efficient in the methods of enhancing their physical assets. Techniques for personal grooming and feminine charms are systematically taught to young French girls as a natural part of the growing up process.

Probing into one's habits of personal beauty rituals is a delicate matter in France, as the women are hesitant to acknowledge or discuss their world-wide reputation as savvy seductresses. They prefer to spend less time talking about the matter and more time applying their skills and reaping the benefits. It is easier to get executives of the fragrance industry to divulge helpful hints about the effective uses of perfume that keep captivated noses on the pleasure trail.

Elegant women in French society are not heavy-handed with application of fragrance, although they somehow have the ability to emit waves of fresh

"If you use this
perfume your
love problems
will vanish."

Jean Honoré
Fragonard
(1732-1806)

blossoms all day without getting caught dabbing on their perfume in public. One of their secrets is their extensive knowledge about the body's pulse points and how these spots and other warm hidden areas are useful in relaying the sweet scents most effectively.

An experienced Frenchwoman can make her presence known by her personalized fragrance formula, and she knows exactly the places on her body to apply the essence for the most lingering effect. Most clues concerning the guarded ritual in applying perfume à la française point to the eighteen key areas of the anatomy that emit the sensuous scents by body temperature and heartbeat.

Daily beauty habits enable Frenchwomen to maintain their hair, skin and nails in the best possible condition, in readiness for any unexpected romantic opportunities that interest them. True femmes fatales will plan meticulously for intimate encounters even though they can give the appearance that a surprise surrender is utterly spontaneous.

The final preparation for a special man begins with a relaxing bath in rich aromatic oils, making certain not to soak in water too long, as the skin must not pucker. Then a light touch of the towel, leaving a slightly moist effect when a scented body lotion is smoothed on from earlobes down to the toes. The fragrance is allowed to set for a few moments, then come the clouds of scented dusting powder to lock in the flavors and coat the skin with a pale angelic finish.

The same fragrance (or a compatible one) is then applied while still in the state of undress by dabbing the pulse points with a generously moistened cotton puff. Key points to consider are:

heels, arches, and between the toes
the inner and outer ankle bone
behind the knees
the underside of the derrière;
the pubic area and the navel
under each breast and between the breasts
the shoulders and upper arms
inside the bend of the elbow
the pulse points at the inner wrist
the back of the hand and between the fingers
the hollow at the bottom of the neck
all around the collar bone
under the chin
along the jaw line
behind the ears and on the earlobes
on the temples
along the back of the neck to the shoulder blades
around the hairline

The process is completed by tucking an aromatic cotton puff inside the bra between the lady's two tender treasures.

The artful application of fragrance takes about fifteen minutes from "bath to blush." However, the time spent promises long range results. Grande dames also saturate their hankies, gloves, scarves and fans with provocative scents to make certain the message that a personality has arrived is perfectly clear. We know

> "Love is a canvas furnished by nature and embroidered by imagination."
>
> Voltaire
>
> (1694-1778)

from the most elementary biology class that nature has made the male animal very susceptible to sensuous female signals through smell.

Women well-versed in "pleasure power" fluff their pillows and sheets with lavender sachets and powders while augmenting the atmosphere with perfumed candles. Delicate copper rings filled with perfumed oils are placed on the top of low voltage light bulbs producing floral or spicy aromas from the warmth of a lighted lamp (pink and apricot tinted lighting provides the most flattering glow to the complexion).

Those who toy with aphrodisiacs know that appealing to the senses does not start and stop with touch alone. To set the stage for sublime moments one can activate all the forces of sight, smell, taste and sound to arouse the anticipation for the final explosion.

Throughout recorded French history appreciation and nourishment of the human senses have been refined arts practiced by seductive women. It is the formula of driving human reactions to the summit that Frenchwomen strive to perfect, never forgetting the importance of a beguiling atmosphere to complete the spell. Rousing the curiosity of an intelligent man with original and provocative details is often neglected by American women who live at a faster pace.

The talent for applying seductive trifles and frivolous minutiae is a category where Frenchwomen are peerless. The hypnotic effect of a shadowy, fragrant atmosphere in a cozy French boudoir is heightened

to the fullest with a few delicate details that play on
the senses. Paris brims with geniuses who excel at
showing off their glorious monuments, bridges and
gardens with lighting effects, and the lessons are not
lost on its private citizens. French hostesses know
exactly how to make a room glow with chandeliers,
sconces and perfumed candles that show off the complexion of beautiful women to full advantage. A man
cannot define all the forces in action; he only knows
that he feels nurtured in the company of a caring
women.

The French embrace many aspects of the modern
world; however, Frenchwomen have no intention of
giving up candlelight just because electricity is abundant, nor do they want to sterilize their abodes
with antiseptic smells.

Disarming an important guest with
a sensuous setting is the first step for
captivating his sentiments.
Good aromas, warm flickering light, sounds of stringed
instruments, and rustling
fabrics set the stage for an award-
winning performance. Add a few
gourmet nibbles and a fine wine, and
the grand prize will be forthcom-
ing before the night is over.

wit and wily wisdom

"It's lovely to
be silly at the
right moment."

Horace
(65-8 B.C.)

able conversation is different at French dinner parties, so different that Americans often
feel left out even when they are bilingual. In
the United States it may be politely suggested not to
agitate the digestive system by discussing sex, politics
or religion. These very subjects, however, are relished
topics at gatherings in France. If the debate about
politics or sex begins to interfere with the process of
eating, a continental hostess will serve up more sooth-
ing subjects like literary trends or current cultural
happenings.

The ability to contribute intelligent, witty conversation at social functions can make or break those
striving to become regulars on the preferred list of
popular Parisian hostesses. Of course, the more lan-
guages one is able to understand, the more cosmo-
politan the playing field becomes.

Whether due to the number of men lost in life's
battles or merely due to the laws of nature, statistics
hold that females are more plentiful in France than
males. Ladies therefore must shine brighter than
male counterparts to make the cut for coveted social
invitations, as socialites on the continent are not fond
of overloading a room with an abundance of superflu-
ous feminine competition. The art of amusing repartee has saved many a plain-featured mademoiselle
from languishing on the lonely sidelines.

Wise French mothers counsel their sons and
daughters on the skills of grace, wit, and amiability.

**"Words really
flattering are not
those which we
propose but those
which escape us
unthinkingly."**

Ninon de L'Enclos
(1620-1705)

The early introduction of these skills in the home
augments French adolescents' rigorous formal education and gives them that rare courtesy, that exquisite
taste, that elegance of deportment and a sense of
moderation in speech that has always distinguished
French sophisticates.

In centuries past when times were less democratic,
unless a woman had a remarkable advantage—such
as holding an influential position in the royal court, a
vast fortune, or incredible beauty—an eligible woman
would have to resort to clever resourcefulness or
extraordinary personal charm to attain a prominent
social standing.

History lessons recounting tales of famous female
achievers have encouraged scores of Gallic damsels
to sharpen their wits and manners. Frenchwomen
often use the lure of coquetry to excite or charm a
male target. They are unrivaled at looking the part
of a demure and proper lady, when underneath that
lacy flounce is a vest of iron with layers of steel-edged
courage.

Clever French women know better than to bore
male suitors with prattle about diets, menopausal suf-
ferings or idle shopping tales. Nor does dialogue on
women's lib often occur in Paris. Women there seem
to be confident about their influence and power
and are more apt to feel discreetly superior to men
rather than subservient. They certainly do not drone
on about sexual harassment or inequality as they
methodically go about taking an equal say in matters
of consequence while striving to correct the laws that

may thwart women.

In lieu of getting steamed up about the equal rights movement which rages in the United States, Frenchwomen spend more energy on subtly maneuvering their lives to suit their desires, both physically and emotionally. The plucky French rarely taint their conversation with dull complaints, and a woman is much more likely to register a doleful appeal for a more active love life than complain about a mundane need for new tires or dental work. It is fascinating to observe how ladies in Paris manage to acquire niceties such as sporty cars, jewelry or a stylish wardrobe while seemingly concentrating on the joys of romance.

Grit with a sugar coating and stoic courage constitute the foundation of a Frenchwoman's fortitude. These women often consider American women pampered citizens having a ridiculously narrow comfort range. When tourists fret about minor inconveniences such as sore feet from unaccustomed walking, jet lag, small closets, or a lack of air-conditioning, the French regard such complaints as childish pleas for attention.

Volumes of advice on the value of lively conversational skills fill French libraries. The Great Love Almanac of 1657 advises youthful aspirants to "secure the latest books and learn how to impart interesting scraps of news and knowledge with a slightly impertinent air." It also suggests that

> **"The height of cleverness is to be able to conceal it."**
>
> Duc de la Rochefoucauld (1613-1680)

"The intellect is always fooled by the heart."

Duc de la Rochefoucauld (1613-1680)

"a lady in the company of men must be free in her speech and say whatever she pleases in order to encourage the ways of Venus."

The wizardry and finesse of Frenchwomen is in knowing how to hold their own among men without obviously arm wrestling the opposite sex to a crushing defeat. In cases when the woman is the more adept of the pair, she may not insist on the last word

but will astutely manage to fit in the last wink, wry smile or pregnant pause. As a prominent Parisian psychiatrist said to me on the subject of female power in France, "the phrase 'she stoops to conquer' says it all."

Popular French hostesses are able to converse knowledgeably on a broad range of topics without playing the part of a pompous prig. They stay current on world politics, philosophy, art, sports, literature, science and smoldering gossip. While it is unlikely that vulgar language will be used, Frenchwomen are quite willing to discuss sex in graphic terms without reservation or giddiness.

The French are masterful at remaining elegant while intentionally stirring up the hormones with provocative conversation or witty innuendoes which may completely bypass less sophisticated members of the group. Women of all ages can cleverly combine smartness, humor and sexuality with cunning agility. An English author, William Shenstone, contends,

"No woman in the world can compete with the Frenchwoman for her power of intellectual irritation. She will draw wit out of a fool."

French erotic language has become extremely rich though their inveterate preoccupation with all forms of love and sentimentality. In the Bibliothèque nationale "erotic subjects" are considered a major category. One finds no less than 300 words listed for carnal acts and over 400 different ways of alluding to one's private parts. The 16th Century court chronicler, Brantôme, wrote that "love-making without words was an imperfect pleasure."

With familiar and regular usage Frenchwomen have become proficient and unflinching in using the language of love. They are able to verbally caress a male prospect in subtle ways that excite him before he has himself thought of romantic intentions. Add to this clever word game the French ability for the fixed gaze, the consummate look, and the admiring stare (eyes for you only), and it becomes an irresistible ploy to ignite a physical flare-up.

In the 17th Century, Voltaire, who was considered one of the all-time great minds in French history, has left us with many explanations for his adoration of clever women and of one woman in particular, Le Marquise du Châtelet.

Gabriel-Emilie du Châtelet was Voltaire's life-long love. He compared her mathematical genius to that of Isaac Newton's. "She was all passion, all mind," Voltaire said. Until her early death at 43, she and Voltaire were devoted companions, living together in

"Charm never fatigues."

André Maurois
(1885-1967)

**"A witty woman
is a devil in
intrigue."**

Molière
(1622-1673)

a union blessed by Emilie's gentle warrior husband, the Marquis du Châtelet.

The Marquis du Châtelet had come from a long line of noble military officers and was an honest and modest man who was proud of his wife's intelligence and seemed happy that she had stimulating company when he was at war. In his social strata, publicly displaying jealousy was simply regarded as bad manners.

In Voltaire's famous memoirs of 1759, he writes, "I found in 1733 a lady who felt more or less as I did, and resolved to spend several years in the country to cultivate her mind, far from the tumult of the world. She was the delight of my life, a woman who had a great disposition for all the sciences. Seldom has so fine a mind and so much taste been united with so much ardor for learning, but she also loved the world and all the amusements of her age and sex. What bound me to her was that each day by her side meant a new discovery, a new enlightenment. She employs all the arts imaginable to captivate me."

Skeptics may cite this famous union as an extraordinary case, but although the Marquise du Châtelet was stellar in her scientific capabilities, she is not unique among the countless Frenchwomen who have had the intelligence and wit to mesmerize brilliant men.

To this day, scintillating repartee is highly prized in French society. Electronic entertainments and mindless parlor games are slow to catch on in a country where human spontaneity and quick wit is revered.

Nightly newscasts are popular in France, but

the population is not obsessed with television. The French are more prone to interact with other human beings and are not content to be mere observers. Whether arguing on the corner, discussing philosophy at the local café or probing hot gossip over a fine meal, the French want to vocalize their thoughts. Sparkling discussions, flirting and naughty banter are by far the preferred adult pastimes. School age children tune in early to nimble word play and quickly become aware that it takes an agile and literate mind to keep up with the mental exercises of interesting people.

Growing up with a solid education in history, the French have a natural proclivity for current politics and the arts, allowing men and women from all social backgrounds to comment coherently on cultural and political events of the day.

"The French have a reputation for extraordinary curiosity and at the same time they have a passion for simple distractions, that refuge of complicated natures," remarks the American author, James Barry.

France is one of the most literate nations in the world. Its colorful history reads better than an adventure story and is a huge part of the curriculum in French school systems. French heritage has primed the French for a life of colorful thoughts and discussions, and they detest being bored. "One must never bore, and therefore one must embellish and provoke with both words and acts," wrote Madame de Graffigny, a popular 18th Century socialite.

"Women are never disarmed by compliments; men always are."

Oscar Wilde
(1856-1900)

french food fantasies

"A good cook is like a sorceress who dispenses happiness."

Elsa Schiaparelli
(1890 - 1973)

"Our cooks rule us," wrote the 19th Century historian, Jules Michelet. Being acutely aware of the pleasure men find in good dining and drinking experiences, Frenchwomen never allow an opportunity to go by that may give them more influence and power over the opposite sex. Leave it to the French to transform the necessity of daily nourishment into "the theater of fine dining."

Pleasure of the palate is another of the senses that women of France have learned to romanticize and to embellish. They have magnified these table tactics to the point of convincing the world that French cooking is highly superior to that of other nationalities. Who can prove or disprove it? The regal reputation of French culinary arts exemplifies centuries of brilliant public relations techniques plus the boundless confidence the French have in their own inherent talents.

Admittedly there is a solid basis for the accolades that France enjoys as cuisine capital of the world. The geographical advantages of fair weather, rich soil, sheltered coastlines, chalky slopes (ideal for champagne grapes) and rolling green pastures have since Roman times made the Gallic regions desirable as a territory which bountifully produces delicious things to eat.

"What miracles
can a wine cup
not work?"

Horace
(65-8 B.C.)

France has been constantly invaded throughout its history by those hoping to possess and govern such a fertile, beautiful and well-situated terrain.

Taking advantage of their good fortune to inhabit the best and most productive regions within European borders, coupled with their devotion to pleasure, it is no wonder the French have developed eating to a high art form. Add to this recipe a generous dose of sexuality that the French appetite craves and you have the makings of a culinary experience that few people can resist.

A Frenchwoman sets the atmosphere for fine dining with a determination to entice all the senses, not just taste alone. She makes certain that succulent aromas fill the air, that shadowy candlelight and a glowing fireplace add warmth, that picturesque china, flatware and fine linens present a feast for the eyes, with fresh flowers to bring nature to the scene, and then she tops it off with good food presented in the most delectable and artistic forms imaginable. Stir into this formula good French wines and a hostess who has only your enjoyment in mind and you have an experience that can transport men to the brink of heaven.

She doesn't forget to permeate the atmosphere with soft digestible music to fill the quiet pauses during the savoring of the divine ambrosia. King Louis XIV had his star musician, Jean-Baptiste Lully, compose special music for his eating events. Lully's Dining Music for the King is still popular in the collections of many classical music enthusiasts.

Lessons in preparing food are paramount to what the French consider a well-rounded education. Even the privileged classes who have little need to toil in the kitchen make an effort to learn the delicate nuances of seasonings, food presentation, creative table settings, and the selection of wines. There is a plethora of priceless lessons available merely by passing the colorful windows of fancy foods at Fauchon's and Hediard's on the Place de la Madeleine in central Paris. The historic Fauchon establishment boasts over 4,000 gourmet foods to study and choose from, artfully displayed, superbly prepared, and ready to take home. One can be assured of the finest and freshest exotic fruits, vegetables, and herbs arranged in eye-catching baskets available even during the off seasons at these pavilions of the palate. If you are, by chance, using an antique 18th Century recipe you will probably be able to find the rare ingredients at Fauchon's or Hediard's.

A memorable eating experience does not depend solely on one's ability to be a gourmet cook, but more on the cleverness of menu, selection of choice meats and vegetables, presentation, warmth of personality, and atmosphere, atmosphere, atmosphere. One can always find in France excellent, prepared delicacies to serve, but it is important to know the right markets, the seasonal specialties, and the most favorable combinations of tastes and colors to complement the sensual setting.

Very few people in France still make their own cheese, but who needs to with over 300 different

> "Love is the greatest refreshment of life."
>
> Picasso
> (1881-1973)

kinds to choose from? The trick in this category is
knowing the perfect look, feel and smell of a ripe
cheese and also the correct temperature for serving.
To see a ripened Camembert just barely oozing out
of its skin on a mild spring day is truly a sensuous
sight. Granted you must have a decently constructed
cheese; still, most of the thrill comes from filling the
senses with an entire scenario of epicurean and visual
delights.

The Great Love Alamac of 1657 gave what was
alleged to be an infallible method of seduction for a
male or female dinner guest: "Take 24 violins, several
turkeys, and fresh green beans (a highly prized dish in
the 17th Century) sweetmeats and splendid costumes.
This medicine should be administered on a fine day,
in pleasant surroundings and agreeable company."

Because fertile lands have provided the Gauls with
abundant agricultural products since the Roman
invasion, food has been an integral component in the
civilization and cultural history of what is now called
France. Eating is often associated with sexual experiences in the ancient love guides that fill an entire sec-
tion of the Bibliothèque nationale in Paris. The French
are supreme at adding theatrics and panache to the
basic needs in life and raising otherwise simple rou-
tines to sublime levels of enjoyment.

Doctor Nicolas Venette's Love Guide of 1696
suggests "should you wish to stimulate your carnal
appetite, you must eat plenty of egg yolks, testicles of
cocks, and shrimps. Little Egyptian crocodiles work
wonders," Doctor Venette assured his readers, "but

they are not easy to procure. However, if you do get them, dried crocodile kidneys pounded into powder and diluted in sweet wine produce excellent results in love making." He advises to wait at least four or five hours after lunch or dinner before making love. He explains that sexual activities immediately after the meal have a bad effect upon the digestion, but he adds that it is equally harmful when one is fasting. His recommendation for the most healthy and vigorous time to make love is at dawn.

If an ambitious French damsel is seriously interested in capturing the attentions of a certain man, she will concoct the most flattering appeal to all his natural appetites: an intimate candlelight dinner prepared by her own tender hands. It is not necessary that the honored guest see the caterer's boxes in the kitchen. All he need be aware of is the aroma from the singular pot on the stove filled with boiling spices and a charming hostess outfitted in flowing fabric to tenderly serve him and sit by his side. Oh, yes, and "would he please take command of pouring the wine."

A memorable meal can be arranged with a little organization, thoughtful menu planning, artistic table setting, two dripless candles, three posies, welcoming smells, low music and gracious attention, plus an ample supply of good wine. Artfully applied, this formula is one that will successfully satisfy the hopes and dreams of almost any diner's appetite.

Don't let financial limitations discourage you from attempting a unique eating experience. A guest will be more likely to remember a magical atmosphere

"The torch of love is lit in the kitchen."

Proverb

and gracious ambiance than the fleeting taste of white truffles. Of course, more imagination must be sprinkled in when it has been a bad season for finances than when the cook has carte blanche at the gourmet market.

During the spartan times of war and occupation in France, citizens kept their spirits up by creating the facsimile of a hospitable hot dinner. If all that could be found was a frail wild rabbit or an old warhorse, at least the creature was served with an important-looking wine sauce and garnished with seasonal chestnuts or currents. A meager pot au feu may be simmering with questionable ingredients, but somehow French cooks manage to add enough window box herbs and roots to give off the smell of a bountiful hearth. Panache is the major spice in most winning French recipes. The nationalistic French have had to put their ingenuity to work to fill in so many cracks in their proud façade that they have become masterful at convincing themselves and the rest of the world of their superior standards for beauty and taste in all things.

The magical salons of the 17th and 18th Century grandes dames that attracted men in droves were not simply gatherings of the affluent, rather they were expertly staged events. An experienced hostess or courtesan would set the scene with the friendly flicker of candelabras, comfortable and cozy seating, a cast of brilliant conversationalists and colorful characters, and then would proceed to provide a tasty menu complete with wine and cigars, while showing her guests the tenderest attention as she rustled about in taffeta and fragile lace. One's mind was kept in active play as the directrice of the household guided the verbal banter through hoops of stimulation and wit.

Whether it is a dinner for two or twenty, set the stage, gather the best food products available, include several à la's when naming the dishes, dress it up, and proceed to put it on stage with the hostess as the accommodating heroine.

If perhaps you do not have access to a setting where your culinary skills can be enacted, leave it to the French to think of all possibilities for the combination of food and romance. Some of the most enchanting restaurants in the world exist in France with no pretense whatsoever to hide the fact that seduction is on the menu.

There are a number of historic restaurants in France that have retained their secluded inside-locking salons for those clients who wish to indulge in a whimsical feast of forbidden fruits. Courtesans and notorious "ladies of leisure" in the 19th Century knew the location of all such hideaways and kept the menus from each establishment in their files so they could preorder suitable selections before arriving with a lover (of course such a woman instinctively knew what would satisfy his hunger better than he did).

Because discretion has always been of prime importance to the French, particularly if they are "well brought up," affairs outside the marriage are not flaunted in public. The private dining rooms in restaurants were kept busy by such notable men and women as Victor Hugo, George Sand, Sarah

Bernhardt, Auguste Rodin and many other well-known personalities where they created passionate afternoons or evenings away from the sanctity of their marital abode. The daring couple would often enter the restaurant separately and meet in one of the reserved salons on the second floor shielded from curious onlookers. The late President Mitterrand was an appreciative client of one historic restaurant near his apartment on the Left Bank.

Laperouse is one of the landmark restaurants in Paris that still offer sentimental lovers a cozy intimate room containing a table for two, a fainting couch and of course, a door which locks from the inside. The ancient hideaway may be a bit faded, but the patina of the wood paneling, the clouded mirrors, and the faded velvet banquettes whisper of the many years when joyful happenings took place in its midst.

After a delicate meal and champagne, the door of the private parlor can be locked and the waiter fore-warned to stay clear of the place unless he hears the bell from inside the den of delights calling for his ser-vices—perhaps to request one final plate of chocolate truffles and a cognac to restore waning energies.

Frenchwomen may have the aura of modesty and coyness about them, but they are unerring when it comes to dropping their veil or their drawers. One can well imagine the erotic effects of amorous adven-tures in a venue that relays the atmosphere of secrecy and the unexpected. Few healthy men would be likely to resist such an epicurean event.

Surely a man who grew up with puritanical sexual

values would be easy prey for such a scene, and would probably float out of the restaurant feeling as if he had visited another world hitherto unknown to him: a gastronomical happening that would pale all previous dining encounters. Thus are provided some inklings into the term femme fatale, because women can be fatal to men when they are adept at creating fantasies of delight for those who have been in the hands of unsophisticated or careless women.

Traditional recipes for French gourmet concoctions can be found in numerous cookbooks and the challenge to succeed is worthwhile for those who love to cook. But if you want "the cooked to be loved," consider the full spectrum of creative French cooking that includes a gener- ous serving of nourish- ment for the soul.

a mention about unmentionables

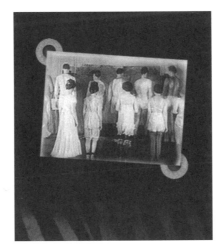

"Good
merchandise, even
when
hidden, soon
finds buyers."

Proverb

Seductive sleepwear and underclothes came into use in France after 1300. Before that time nightclothes and underwear were practical, worn simply to stay warm in drafty stone castles and unheated dank dwellings. These rough heavy garments were removed, or not removed, depending on the piety of the partner, for the purposes of propagating.

In common usage during the middle ages was the chemise cagoule, a coarsely woven nightshirt, purposefully uncomfortable but with a suitably placed hole through which the husband could impregnate his wife. This method satisfied those who associated chastity with holiness and were confused whether the physical act was good for their soul or for that matter whether they should even think of the event with pleasure.

When bands of singing troubadours and traveling poets began to appear on the scene, sentiment and romance slowly became more popular and warmed up the chilly attitude about lovemaking. Before that the Church Fathers promoted copulation for the purpose of propagation only and frowned upon the sexual act in association with desire, pleasure or romance. It was not until the 11th Century that the arts of love and sentiment began to flourish with the French, whose romantic techniques until that time were far more primitive than those of the civilized world in the Orient. But with the appearance of the colorful troubadours romance began to blossom, then soar, and a whole new exuberance surged up between the sexes.

The first widely recorded troubadour was Duc Guillaume IX of Aquitaine (1071 - 1127), the grandfather of Queen Eleanor of Aquitaine. This handsome and courageous Duke returned from his military campaign in Spain bringing with him the Moorish singers and minstrels who had delighted him with provocative poetry, songs and sensuous dances during the year-long crusade against the Moors.

Duc Guillaume saw Northern Europe as a fertile region in which to sow the love buds of romance after the inhabitants had lingered so many years in the dreary Dark Ages. During the grim and austere era following the downfall of the Roman occupation in 476 A.D., human sentimentality was at a particularly low ebb and physical encounters were often of the lusty carnal nature or reserved for the practicality of adding more children to help with the workload. Clothing reflected the severity of the mood and was styled in simple mundane designs and somber colors.

The Franks were poised and ready for a renaissance and when the notion of sentimental love and chivalry was brought to Paris by the troubadours. They reacted with enthusiasm. The geographical location presented an ideal setting for romance offering a temperate climate that encouraged moonlight meetings, frolicking in the haystacks and meadows, and embracing on the beautiful Atlantic beaches. The Frankish language spoken with pouty lips was suited to the soft expressive words and songs of adoration. Their reverence of natural or applied aesthetics, even though long subdued, was primed to burst out with a curiosity for sensual pleasures.

As the troubadours traveled from the castles to the town festivals with their amusing and entertaining messages of courtly love, the arts of courtship gained immediate popularity among the nobles and aristocrats.

The Fathers of the Roman Catholic Church were alarmed by all this "frivolous debauchery" which took leisure time activities away from praying, chastity observances, and worshiping in holy places. Writing in his Livres de Manières in 1170, Étienne Fougères, chaplain to King Henry II of England, accused the queen and wealthy ladies of France of "provoking wars and jealous feuds, of adultery, fornication and abortion."

However, after tasting the delights of ars amandi (arts of love), the French became eternal addicts of the game of romance and soon were known as the acknowledged leaders in that field, a position from which they have never been ousted.

Soon after the pious era of King Saint Louis, who

> "Though modesty is a virtue, yet bashfullness is a vice."
>
> Proverb

died in 1270, the attitudes about sexual pleasures changed quickly and radically, indicating that the Franks were eager to respond to the messages of the jolly troubadours. Their instinctively sensual temperments were well-suited to the new lessons of love.

The metal chastity belts that the early crusaders had locked on their wives before leaving home for the Holy Land began to seem outdated and severe. With the concurrence of knights, courtly flirtations and chivalry, a social code arose which was guided by honor and courtesy even though the mannerisms were often stilted and theatrical.

Courtly love, called enamorment, became the rage and was described as "beginning with the eyes which produced a state of ecstasy releasing an ethereal fluid transmitted from the eyes to the heart where it engendered love."

The competition among the aristocratic ladies for eye-catching and seductive apparel began heating up during this focus on sensual beauty. Women's busts were no longer bound up and hidden under drab garments. Agnes Sorel, the brazen yet devoted mistress of Charles VII (1403-1461) was said to have the most beautifully shaped breasts in the kingdom of France. Quite conscious of her mammary superiority, she introduced a new, shocking style of "bare to the waist" dresses at court. Later she became more sophisticated and subtle, choosing to display only one breast, a fashion recorded in many paintings of her era. One of the well-known masterpieces that the lovely Agnes posed for is the intriguing "La Vierge

de Melun" by Fouquet which is now owned by the
Museum of Anvers. It was suitable for public display
because Fouquet depicted the King's mistress as the
Virgin Mother Mary nursing the baby Jesus in her
arms.

Most damsels who did not have the honor of sharing the bed of the King were somewhat less courageous in their wearing apparel, only daring to show
their cleavage at the top of richly jeweled necklines,
just covering their nipples. They laced up their corsets so tight that their breasts burst out under their
chins so that "a candlestick could be placed upon
them."

Through the ages French women have developed
a wise understanding about keeping parts of the body
demurely hidden from view, while displaying merely
a "peek" with amusing finesse. Jacques d'Amiens' love
guide of the Middle Ages advises his readers to "curtain oneself with sheer cloth before a lover enters the
bedchamber, and do not dress in front of one's lover,
for he might see some detail that he does not approve
of."

Marguerite of Navarre, the beloved sister of the
French King Henri II, described in one of her many
journals a lady sitting up in bed in a lace nightcap
and a nightgown "covered with pearls and precious
stones," an outfit that creates a lovely picture but
sounds rather uncomfortable for sleeping. Nightcaps
stayed in fashion until the 19th Century and were
worn by both men and women to complete the
proper night ensemble while providing a convenient

"All fashionable
vices pass for
virtue."

Molière
(1622-1673)

way to stay warm during the freezing damp winters.
Ladies of the 16th Century began to take a
great interest in fancy undergarments. Panties were
invented about 1530 at Queen Catherine de Medici's
request, as she preferred to ride sidesaddle to show off
her shapely legs and needed protection from her billowing skirts on windy days.

One would think moralists of the day would
approve of the new knickers, called calçons, however,
they did not. One journalist of court wrote, "Women
should leave their buttocks uncovered under their
skirts. They should let their behinds remain nude as
is suitable for their sex." Others like Henri Estenni
approved of the new garment saying, "These calçons
are useful to keep women tidy, prevent the onslaught
of dust and cold and furthermore stop them from
showing too much of their body when they fall from
a horse. They also afford a measure of protection
from disrespectful men who, when they slide their
hand under a lady's skirt will no longer come into
direct contact with her flesh."

The exaggerated basket skirts, or paniers, with
wishbone hoops worn by Madame de Pomadour,
Madame du Barry, and Marie Antoinette in the 1700's
were certainly not made for comfort, but to give the
illusion of enveloping a precious store of sweet fruits
underneath. Men of the court would linger at the
base of the grand staircases at Versailles to watch the
majestic descents of the noble ladies in these cre-
ations in order to catch one thrilling revelation of a
tiny satin-clad foot peeking out from under the tilting

silk and satin hoops.

In 1850 Empress Eugenie popularized the crinoline underskirts made from yards and yards of taffeta,
organdy and lace to be worn under the billowing
velvet skirts that were in vogue. Connoisseurs judged
the rank and education of lady visitors to Eugenia's
court simply from the way in which they managed
their crinoline skirts when they were about to sit on
a cushioned tabouret. There was usually a gathering
of eager young dandies who placed themselves at
the approach to the Opera Garnier's marble staircase
so they could observe the grand ladies lift the "froth
of frills" as they were about to scale the steps. They
could be satisfied with a mere glimpse of the long
white ruffled pantalons which anchored the layers of
quivering organdy petticoats.

Not much has changed about the delights of
forbidden sights except for the fact that there is so
much less that is denied now that the thrill is more
difficult to come by. After one has revealed all, the
arts of intrigue often resort to strange props and exercises. Frenchwomen cleverly have managed to retain
some of the secrets of tantalizing peeks, glimpses, and
provocative revelations with the help of imaginative
French lingerie.

Most career-minded American women have given
up the hassle with garters and thigh-high hosiery, opt-
ing for the practicality of panty hose. French ladies
often forego the quick ease of panty hose for the
provocative femininity of garters and stockings which
they do not consider a deviant item, but merely

"more alluring." Paris boutiques still proudly display myriads of choices in colorful garterbelts and lace-trimmed stockings with all kinds of matching teddies, panties, bras and other intimate paraphernalia. Judging from the plentiful inventory in fashionable Paris shops, Europeans, whether men or women, are maintaining a healthy demand for luxury lingerie.

I do not profess to be privy to the techniques of exactly how French women put the luxurious undies to use; however, I did have the opportunity to interview the descendant of Hermionie Cadolle, the 19th Century French seamstress who designed one of the most liberating bras of her era. After five generations Poupie Cadolle continues the family tradition of operating the exclusive custom lingerie business which caters to a thriving clientele in an upscale silk and velvet-lined store near the Ritz Hotel in Paris.

Although her entire afternoon agenda was booked up with private fittings, Poupie appeared relaxed, charming and full of humor and warmth. Her feminine and stylish appearance along with her sparkling personality is indicative of how she likes her sensuous designs to be worn, with a relaxed girlish air that is balanced by an attitude of sophisticated amusement.

Cadolle's shop has an illustrious list of clients with more than 5,000 personalized patterns on file that include those of Catherine Deneuve, the late Princess Diana, Madonna, Brigitte Bardot, The Duchess of Windsor, Mata Hari and most of the top international models who come to Paris for the spring and fall couture fashion shows.

Poupie keeps several historic patterns of famous courtesans and actresses of the Belle Époque in her valuable archives. She extols the glamour of the famous courtesan, Liane de Pougy, who was still beautiful and romantically active well into her sixties. Madame de Pougy continued her acting career into the 20th Century, then chose to leave it behind to marry Prince Ghika and become a titled princess. Stories of her magnificent jewelry collection have filled many biographies, but suffice to say that she had extravagant emerald toe rings designed to match her mint green nightgowns which only a few privileged men were allowed to see.

"Frenchwomen have a strong sense of independence," said Poupie, "but they do not feel they lose their individuality by wearing the color or style of intimate apparel that their lovers like or suggest. Ladies in France enjoy pleasing men as well as themselves and do not in the least consider themselves subservient when they wear provocative undies."

Frenchwomen find it pleasing to wear lovely lingerie to augment their own feeling of femininity and self-esteem. They do not save glamorous lingerie for a "special occasion," always leaving the element of surprise concerning the happenstance of an ultimate moment. They prefer a spontaneous attitude and do not like to think in terms of a planned agenda for "lovemaking" (the term preferred in France to "having sex"). The elements of surprise and spontaneity are highly prized in almost any game among the cultivated French population.

Madame Cadolle finds that her American customers are usually more practical when buying lingerie and choose more blacks and nude colors to go with everything, rather than the pretty blues, pinks, reds and lily white satin that Frenchwomen primarily choose.

"It is quite obvious that Frenchwomen are more comfortable with their bodies than American women are," said Poupie. "They are not embarrassed by an extra pound of flesh here and there and have few qualms about enjoying physical love at any age." It is known however that they like to hold on to their own secrets of allure and hesitate to give out personal information about such things as their favorite seamstress, masseuse, hairdresser, plastic surgeon, or lingerie shop.

French lingerie is traditionally revered for the quality of the silky, soft and slinky satin and charmeuse fabrics, the delicate trims, workmanship and body-hugging fit. One can pay a high price for the finer pieces, but a unique frothy item can be worth millions in pleasurable rewards. The custom-made pieces can last for years with good care and the avoidance of too much rigorous tugging and pulling upon them. Even during lovemaking, the French say that one must wear a bit of clothing, "very little, if you like, but something."

Cadolle's shop has a great many men who order gifts on a regular basis. "They usually have very good taste," she said, "preferring feminine pastel colors and a form-fitting garment, and not always the terribly naughty numbers, but the more suggestive items, like teddies and camisoles." Poupie recommends shopping for lingerie with a man, as they are perfectly frank about what looks good on a woman they like and are willing to pay for the more extravagant styles.

The Cadolle staff emphasizes that they keep their accounts very discreet and have never had a mix-up between the wife and the mistress of the same man. "We French are not so traditionally puritanical as Americans. We treat the intrigues of love practices as a part of nature."

Just as nature adorns the birds of paradise with colorful and appealing plumage, so do the French lingerie designers adorn their lovebirds for the wonders and pleasures of life.

living well with less

"The manner of giving is worth more than the gift."

Pierre Corneille (1606-84)

 recurring observation that fascinates count-less American women who visit France is the ability of the French general population to appear stylish and affluently dressed at all social and income levels.

It is understandable that the wealthy can take advantage of the famous designer boutiques that line the avenues of Paris, but the mystery is how the working girls can afford to look so chic in this very expensive city while they exist on meager salaries. Certainly there are some generous men left in the world who are willing to help attractive ladies enjoy the luxuries of life while the men benefit from a beautifully dressed trophy on their arm.

Actually these convenient alliances are not as read-ily available in our more conservative times; none the less, one sees vast numbers of middle income women in Paris who dress as if they had carte blanche to the best couture houses in town. In reality most of the young women who display a chic flare in their appearance manage to do so on frugal budgets and uncanny confidence. How do they do it?

Looking splendid and well-cared for on a spartan budget is yet another talent that French females carry off with imperturbable

"Life is made up
of little things."

Proverb

self-assurance. There is, of course, the definite advantage in possessing a discerning eye for quality and style that comes from years of exposure to the resplendent store windows lining the Paris streets. The inhabitants of Paris are bombarded with lessons in aesthetics every day they venture out their front door whether they live in a posh neighborhood or a simple working class area.

During a casual afternoon stroll, one can encounter boutique windows with tapestries made by Gobelins, fine laces from Alençon, luxurious silks from Lyon, sensational jewels from Cartier, couture clothing from Christian Dior and display windows exhibiting world class antique furniture.

The recognition of quality begins at an early age in France whether one is brought up in a home filled with Baccarat chandeliers and Christofle silver or whether the opportunity to learn about fine workmanship comes from viewing sophisticated public displays. Some of the most exquisite treasures in the world are readily accessible to the average Parisian merely if he keeps his mind and eyes open.

By the time an alert French schoolgirl reaches the age of sixteen, she is able to zero in on a fragment of hand-made lace in a pile of second-hand castoffs, or she can burrow into a dingy box of miscellaneous items and pull out a crushed Schiaparelli felt hat. Such an enigmatic talent for discovering a gem can be maddening to an American like me who has recently gone through the same carton unaware of the prize piece waiting to be found.

Parisian career girls have an uncanny sense that beams in on tarnished but revivable craftsmanship. Then after uncovering a discarded treasure they are resourceful about repairing the frayed edges and moth-holes until the garment or object returns to a useful life. Reports from several sources indicate that this knack to rehabilitate used merchandise to a state of new potential applies equally well to pumping new life into a broken-down man.

France is a nation which has learned through many hard lessons of war how to be frugal and how not to waste at any social level. Fine vintage linens are handed down from generation to generation and mended over and over again. Grandmother's damask handtowels are coveted even though a row of braid must be added to conceal the tattered edges. The chipped rims on antique crystal are expertly ground smooth by artisans with equipment dating from the last century. It is as if this reverence for pure hand-wrought craftsmanship is a proud national hobby.

In many instances French working women possess the taste for designer clothing as well as a discerning eye for wearing it well, but often do not have the bank account to go along with the desire. In reality, less than one percent of the world's population buys classic haute couture at the retail prices shown at elegant fashion houses on Avenue Montaigne and Rue Saint Honoré (the publicity and excitement generated by these expensive designs sell the perfumes and accessories which support the couture industry).

Smart Frenchwomen in all income strata have a list

> "Love will find a way."
>
> Proverb

"Little goods, little care."

Proverb

of obscure clothing outlets where they can find end-of-season items or leftovers from last year's collections at less than half the original cost. It may take some research to locate these nondescript establishments, but finding them is worth the effort.

Chic Parisians are fairly guarded about their off-price resources for designer clothing and usually do not discuss how they acquire their wardrobe, particularly with mere acquaintances. You may be lucky enough to get a hot tip from a friend who is a model or from a journalist who is on a press list and receives notices of the sales by mail.

It is unlikely that prestigious designers will publically advertise sample sales, so be ready to take the opportunity to go to a private sale if someone invites you to go along. Try to find at least one item at the bargain event that suits you and be sure to pay by credit card or check so your mailing address can be added to the client list. Once you are considered a customer and make an occasional purchase, you will probably receive notices of seasonal sell-offs for several years.

If you are modest, timid or intimidated by aggressive crowds, be forewarned, sales in the wholesale district could upset your equilibrium. The end-of-collection events in November or June start about nine in the morning for a two- or three-day period. The line begins to form about an hour before the doors open and consists of savvy career girls, society mavens, chic models, and boutique owners, most of whom are aware of what goes on inside and are dressed for action. Wear something casual that is easy to pull off and on and decent underwear because there are rarely secluded areas to try on garments in the large warehouse loaded with racks of merchandise.

Only a limited number of people are allowed in at one time, but before long the scene is a confusing mess with piles of articles stacked everywhere while half-dressed women (and sometimes men) plow through the jungle of clothes vying for a look in one of the sparsely placed mirrors. If your nerves can handle the spectacle, the prices for superior quality couture pieces are well worth the fuss.

Stock levels are a matter of chance, as deliveries from the posh retail shops are sent at irregular intervals. Many of the off-price outlets are listed in insider shopping guides, or can be tracked down if one asks enough questions; however, they are often located on side streets away from the high priced tourist haunts, so take a map when on the quest for warehouse sales.

Besides their secret sources for bargain couture clothing, Frenchwomen possess a keen talent for combining colors and accessories that can make hand-me-downs look stellar. They can utilize a luxurious Hermes scarf for decades, somehow making it look different each season by tying it in a hundred feminine ways and letting it flutter in the breeze while leaving a trail of perfume in its wake. (Hermes has a sale at least once a year, privately advertised).

Even the most modest paychecks seem to allow for a splurge on at least one luxury garment per season and Frenchwomen soon build a wardrobe

"Nothing is impossible to a willing heart."

Proverb

**"More than
enough is too
much."**

Proverb

of attractive belts, scarves, blouses, hats, gloves, and
costume jewelry geared to add zest to the most basic
ensembles. Almost every French coquette eventually
manages to acquire an impressive piece of knockout
jewelry, perhaps an inherited treasure or a lover's gift.
Although it may be the most valuable piece in her
possession, you can be certain that she will muster
the courage to wear it with aplomb whether it shows
up on a casual sweater or on a velvet cocktail suit.
The message is meant to relay: "Nothing unusual
here; I am accustomed to fine things."

These subtle nuances of savoir-faire that make
less look like more, are carried out so quietly that the
total stylish appearance makes it difficult to judge
between frugal fashion and actual affluence. Herein
lies another clue to the French mystique, the ability
to make a well-thought- out plan, menu or outfit,
look elegant yet effortless.

Many grande dames in France dwell in impressive
inherited châteaux or large, richly furnished apartments, but they have little income to maintain a
comfortable cash flow. Often these elegant premises
are chilly in the winter while the inhabitants adjust
by wearing extra layers of clothing rather than turning up the heat and paying high heating bills. Lights,
ovens and other appliances are used thoughtfully
with regard to the high cost of electricity, an expense
that can be shocking in France.

Centuries of invasions and occupations have taught
the French how to conserve food wisely and cre-
atively. Yesterday's baguette is made into toasted crou-

tons. Beef bones flavor the brewing pot au feu, while calves' tongue and brains, and pigs' nose and ears are imaginatively turned into delectable delicacies.

It would take a translation of family recipe files to disclose what flavorful remnants can be puréed to produce French exotic sauces and soups. One must admire the French ability to earn the reputation as the "cuisine capital of the world" while still remaining masters of frugality. One can only speculate on the various ingredients and processes utilized in making the 355 known cheeses of France.

Still the people of France do not lack generosity of spirit or extravagance when it comes to aesthetics. They have distinct priorities and are willing to spend liberally on bountiful flower arrangements, rare wine or choice ingredients for a memorable dining experience. They will go beyond routine measures to secure the best products available and often squirrel away their notebooks of secret addresses where quality exists at favorable prices.

With endless clever shortcuts and astute management many noble people of France can circumvent the cash flow problem with dignity, and the lifestyle of a discerning Parisian can appear far more enviable than flashy and frivolous creatures on big spending allowances in other parts of the world.

There is a brand of confident women in France who possess a basic sense of refined judgement that allows simplicity to translate into elegance while they function admirably in a modest manner. This type carries the air of blue-blood heritage and has the abil-

"Thrift is good
revenue."

Proverb

ity to make up for lack of funds with an abundance
of charm, sincerity and warmth and invariably will
welcome her guests with genuine graciousness and
make the effort to provide them with the best of
everything she has available.

In Anne Conover's Caresse, it is said of one society
hostess who had outlasted her inheritance that "she
always put on high face and high table, even if she
had little food to serve. She could make a Renaissance
meal out of a package of soup and a poetry reading."

All too often, entertaining with flair is equated to
lavish budgets. Certainly one can be more generous
on a grander scale with copious coffers but there can
occur a great respect for a creative individual who
exudes refinement merely with a proud presence, a
stem of sherry and a plate of pâté.

It is the the French elite of noble character, living
on modest means, but with a sense of the sublime,
who are inspirational in creating the fantastic from
mere fragments.

Sturdy and proud citizens are numerous in France,
as the country has learned well in their 2000 year history of social extremes. The gentry can be feasting on
cake, while the tax-paying peasants are rioting for a
loaf of bread. However, even when the circumstances
are reversed, the crafty French triumph. They deal
with either end of the spectrum with stoic dignity.

alone or not to be

"Loneliness can
be conquered only
by those who can
bear solitude."

Proverb

Women must consider the possibility that they may not always have an ideal roommate, a compatible traveling companion, or a delightful dinner partner. Statistically women are destined to outlive their male counterparts, but even before the grim reaper narrows the field, there are continual complaints concerning the paucity of desirable male companions.

As today's women grow more comfortable with their newly-found freedoms and their ability to travel solo, they have become far more selective about whom they allow to invade that precious independence.

In France, singleness is managed with remarkable dignity by both men and women. European females have had practical lessons in getting along admirably without an escort by their side. From the earliest era of the Crusades in the Middle Ages when much of the male population left on pilgrimages to the Holy Land that took four or five years, up until this century when two World Wars wiped out huge numbers of fathers, husbands, sons and brothers, the women left on the homefront learned to cope independently with fierce determination.

It is debatable whether the stoic composure of solitary European females comes from a true sense of confidence or whether it is a proud façade. In either case, the message of unaccompanied Frenchwomen is effective in portraying a self-reliant person who knows what she wants and how to get it. The notable level of satisfaction along with the strength and determination of this authoritative aura adds to the French mystique and spurs the curiosity and envy of those who feel inadequate when left on their own.

The remarkably low suicide rate in France and the rare demand for tranquilizers or sex therapy, as well as the lack of interest in "lonely hearts clubs" leads one to believe that there is validity in the reputation for self-assurance that the French are said to possess.

Lone Gallic women, whether widowed, divorced or celibate by choice, generally do not carry the look

of rejection. It stands to reason that rational, successful men are more apt to be attracted to a woman who savors life rather than a sheepish-looking reject or a shrinking violet. Verve and vitality contribute to personal magnetism, a winning combination that French women have perfected through the ages.

While dining alone at a restaurant, a Frenchwoman can appear downright smug and pleased with her situation. If the picture is a typical one, the lady will be stylishly dressed for a night out and will have a well-mannered dog lying attentively at her feet. Her banquette against the wall will be well-chosen for a vantage point from which to scrutinize other diners, and although appearing somewhat aware of those around her, she will display the demeanor of one far too content with her own company to long for an intruder. The good wine, a tasty meal, her loyal pooch, and a solicitous waiter are sufficient, thank you.

To assure friendly service when dining alone, one needs to avoid small intimate establishments with fewer than 20 tables, as every place setting in small cafés is calculated to turn a profit. Bright, lively restaurants like Brasserie Lipp, Le Balzar and La Coupole, or hotel salons are good choices for singles, unless of course, one is a regular at a favorite local haunt. If the lady is famous or has frequented the place for decades, she may have rights to her chosen table and all house rules are abandoned. It is perfectly permissible to order demi-bottles of wine, but be gracious enough to order enough delicacies from the menu to justify the use of the table and view.

Ordinarily it is difficult to pierce the aloofness of an unaccompanied French lady, as friendliness to strangers is not a familiar habit of the reserved French. One notable exception is an irrepressible comment about the adorableness of an owner's pet pup. Heart-felt enthusiasm about one's dog is considered an acceptable ice-breaker. The nation invariably allows preferential treatment to its canine citizens irrespective of breed, and Frenchwomen are particularly well served by their precious pooches when it comes to altering strict etiquette guidelines.

A sensitive lady can send subtle clues of her warmth and tenderness merely by the way she holds, grooms and whispers to her beloved pet. It is ingenious how these darling animals can be taught to relay the message that to be loved by their mistress is a sublime experience.

A faithful dog can watch over his owner while perched in a backpack, swinging in a Louis Vuitton pet purse, or strutting at the end of an Hermes leather leash. His head rests contentedly on her foot while she has tea, or he waits longingly while staring at her through the window of the butcher shop. When she dines in a café, doggie may sleep blissfully with his head on her lap, thus luring a man's thoughts to wonder if his head would ever be so welcomed in that cozy position.

Frenchwomen and their furry friends have developed a subtle art of flirting with the outside world, using such masterful adroitness that people who fall into the spell are scarcely aware that they are a target. The unexpected methods of coquetry such as the "pampered pet" lure perpetuate the illusive reputation of the femme fatale.

Probing stares are unashamedly exchanged at the best brasseries in Paris. Leave it to the Italians to talk with their hands; the French are the undeniable masters of sending signals by eye contact. Perfectly proper ladies have few qualms about taking a visual inventory of any person they find interesting, and they carry off the obvious observation with unabashed pleasure. It is pointless to try to outstare a Frenchwoman when she is in her own territory, nor should you give any signs of being intimidated whether you are a man or a woman. If the French find you worthy of anything more than a passing glance, you can consider it a compliment. The "meaningful look" is a perfected art in France.

The visual message at which Frenchwomen excel is not so elementary as a "come hither" gesture; that's too overt for a sophisticated coquette, unless she is actually in the business of procurement. Usually the admiring look will leave a question as to the point of focus—whether the lady across the room is observing the attractive man or the painting behind him. Secretly, of course, he fantasizes that he is the target of interest and his curiosity has been aroused. There are few peacocks who can resist flattering attention.

If the spark can be kindled, the man in question will devise a courteous approach, perhaps by sending a drink to her table or by commenting on her dog as he quietly passes her table. If he is the chivalrous sort, he will not indicate that he saw her watchful eye, but instead that he noticed her from the moment she entered the room.

Women keeping their own company in France traditionally comport themselves with heads held high, even if they are existing at the moment on a reduced income. They detest appearing desperate or pitiful and they manage to put themselves together in a cared-for fashion no matter what the status of their finances.

Women in France have far too much pride to resort to the down and out approach when on the

lookout for a mate or mentor. They can conjure up much more imaginative bait than pity to entice a man into providing them with the necessary luxuries to make their life more comfortable.

Frenchwomen have the knack of tracking down quality pieces to wear giving little regard to a few threadbare cuffs or buttonholes. The important issue to relay is the appreciation and recognition of the finer things. It is more likely that a true gentleman will become fascinated with the unique elegance of a stylish creature rather than become concerned with a few frayed edges on her couture jacket.

There are fewer men these days who have the time, the money or the patience to dedicate to taking a waif off the street and turning her into a polished glamour girl, as in the tale of Doctor Higgins and Eliza Doolittle in My Fair Lady. A girl in today's world will be better served to present herself nicely packaged in order to ignite a relationship rather than someone in need of charity.

European women are renowned for making widowhood or singleness look like an enviable state of being, with no hint whatsoever of yearning for a partner. They bring dignity to the status of solitude and can make it appear genuinely appreciated. Widows and divorcées in France are able to disguise any obvious signs of dire need or rampant lust with aplomb. It seems that a hot pursuit usually makes wild horses and eligible men gallop in the opposite direction, and it is the softer approach that seems to disarm men upon first meeting a woman.

Many solitary Parisians talk a convincing story about finding Paris itself stimulating enough for a fulfilling love affair. They sing the praises of such a love—Paris as paramour is handsomely groomed, always waiting, full of surprises, culturally tantalizing, ready to answer any whim, offers gourmet delicacies at every turn, and is forever ready with stellar sights, sounds and smells to produce moments of epiphany.

Ninon de L'Enclos (1620-1705), a woman celebrated for her individuality and beauty, was one of the first well-known rebels of the tyranny of possessive husbands. After an enlightened education by a proud and brilliant father, she made no secret of her conviction that marriage was not included in her life plan. She established herself in the literary district in Paris near Place des Vosges and reigned for 50 years over a dazzling salon where she received a distinguished mix of nobles, politicians, artists and writers, many of whom she took as lovers.

Ninon was an advocate of free love, taking remarkable men as lovers. but was unable to stay loyal to a monogamous affair for much longer than six months at a time. She remarked that, "Nothing in nature is more varied than the pleasures of love, even though it is so much the same."

Her famous salon was sought after as a finishing
school for young men who were sent there by their
fathers for a "manly education." She was able to extol
the graces of love and at times share the actual experience of the flesh with young lovers in an atmosphere
of elegance, literary conversation and social refinement. Evidently her ability to entice men was well-
developed enough to attract lovers of all ages until she
was well into her seventies.

Fascinating history lessons like that of the life of
Ninon de L'Enclos help the French soften the imag-
ined fears of being single or growing old. In praise
of solitude is a common theme in French literature;
in fact, an impressive number of famous intellects
agreed with the lifelong bachelor, Voltaire, who said,
"Marriage is the only adventure open to the coward-
ly."

There is an arrogance that persists among the
French clan which makes living alone in their revered
city of Paris appear to be utopia and clearly the
choice status of the intellectual. The French are able
to thrive happily with their own company and rarely
refer to the state of loneliness. Not to say, mind you,
that a French lady ever closes her mind to passionate
encounters, but there exists a time when obsession
with the chase has cooled and one becomes more
content with a solo flight into passions of the more
cerebral type.

A woman portraying this message of well-being is
often the very spark that attracts busy, successful men

who are looking for an element of confidence and stability in their own hectic lives.

of a certain age

There comes a satisfying time in an intelligent woman's lifetime when she has reached a lofty level of practical knowledge concerning the facts of life and has managed to retain an inner glow of beauty that still attracts admirers with whom she can continue to learn and polish her abilities.

The phrase "a certain age" has appeared in French conversation and writings for hundreds of years. Dr. Lillian Rubin, author of Women of a Certain Age: The Midlife Search for Self, says that women in this category can enjoy the confidence and wisdom of experience to make the years from fifty and beyond emotionally rewarding. The early use in England of this term referred to spinsterhood, but the French often think of women of a certain age as those sensual females who have lived a half of a century or more and are willing to gracefully impart their wisdom to initiate young men and boys into the pleasures of love.

In France, discretion is held in high regard, and the French find few circumstances important enough to ask a woman's age. After she obviously has passed the legal drinking age and beyond the time when one must consider whether she is a delicate virgin, a

"There's many a
good tune played
on an old fiddle."

Proverb

Frenchwoman doesn't trifle with specifics concerning age. Nor do her admirers.

Paris can be a very agreeable place to live for those women who can no longer base their appeal on the dewy freshness of youth. France prides itself on being considered a cerebral nation where one can succeed by wit and cleverness, as well as a polished sense of style. With a capacity for passion and a knack for witty conversation one never need become an old lady in France, but can be admired as a vital individual from the time one attains womanhood until the deathbed. With finesse, a coquette can be ageless, allowing romance to remain in her life until the last satisfied sigh.

It has to do with the daily practice of the French to strive for mental alertness and verbal dexterity and their sincere belief in the ensuing benefits. The ideal code of existence for most French citizens encompasses self-respect, dignity, curiosity, pride, romance and style. The typical Frenchwoman tends to resist any physical barriers that get in the way of this pattern for a gracious and happy life.

The aggrandizement of years is graciously looked upon as a sublime wealth of experience that mature women are willing to impart upon a few lucky souls, worthy of the largess. The long standing tradition stemming from the times of the royal courtiers leads one to believe that the fortunate men selected to become privy to the tender knowledge gathered by a mature woman are in for wondrous delights and valuable secrets.

The myth seems to have a fairly sturdy foundation. After surveying innumerable romances of famous mature courtesans and their devoted young lovers, one's curiosity about the power of those women of a certain age becomes heightened. Evidently there is enough hard evidence behind the reputation of masterful mavens to attract many present-day lovers to the boudoirs of seductresses who would have long been considered over the hill if living in an American society.

Jules Michelet, a chronicler in the 19th Century, advised a young lover, "Our hearts are not yet tender in early age. To achieve love, one needs time, one must have been tested by adversities. One must love long and faithfully before the heart acquires grace. Real youth begins later in life. You are not young, Madame, but you are on you way to becoming young."

He also believed that "adolescents are more cold-hearted than they fancy themselves. They mistake every passing desire for love. Temperament, hot-bloodedness, these they mistake for tenderness."

Honoré de Balzac had many mistresses during his 51 adventurous years in the 19th Century, and almost every one of his paramours was older than he was. He made good use of their experiences and confidences, as his writing expertly displays when he describes appealing mature female characters. Balzac's famous heroine, Madame de Girordin, observed, "our young girls are too concerned with making a rich match—

> "Forty is the old age of the youth; fifty is the youth of old age."
>
> Proverb

passion comes to them later."

In the 16th Century, the famous seductress, Diane
de Poitiers, was 20 years older than her ardent lover,
King Henri II, who showered her with honor, riches,
and respect for 30 years until his untimely death at
41 in a jousting accident. To this day, Diane de Poitiers
remains a muse of love and beauty for women of all
ages, but particularly for those struggling with the
aging process.

The spell that Diane cast over the popular King
was so great that she had to constantly deny that she
used sorcery and magic potions to hold his attentions.
Most history books attest to her legendary talents
of seduction, enormous energy and mental vitality,
beauty techniques and humor. Royal chroniclers
focus on her expert skill as a horsewoman which the
King greatly appreciated, as he was an accomplished
hunter himself and loved nature as she did. They also
extol Diane's feminine allure and cool common sense
that exerted a total fascination over the King for the
last three decades of his life.

Diane de Poitiers relays a timely message in her
writings when she records that no matter how
devoted Henri might be to her charms, she knew
that if she were to hold the devotion of a handsome,
virile young man, who was also the King of France,
she would need to continue to sharpen her skills of
romance, magic, amusements, and excitement, "plus
more," she said.

To help defy time and minimize the difference in
their ages, wherever she was, Diane created an envi-

ronment in which Henri could be his natural self and
at peace with the world. Surrounded by an almost
magical aura of youthfulness, Diane arranged amusing
games, festivals, hunting banquets and fanciful distractions for her lover. She carefully contrived to enthrall
this energetic man by pleasing all his desires while
continually interjecting newness into each experience. Diane de Poitiers was a sublime enchantress
and Henri was her willing captive.

Even though Frenchwomen base their magnetic
spell over men primarily on mental fascination, their
sensible and regular beauty habits have paid off for
females of all ages. They consider lifelong care and
healthful treatment of the body more important
than the application of layers of concealing makeup
Their so-called "natural" look plays a big part in their
earthy femininity and lusty attractiveness. The girlish
disarray of a dangling curl or uncontrollable wisps of
hair slightly mussed lipstick and other nonchalant
imperfections often captivate American men who are
accustomed to seeing women too perfectly made up
and relaying an intimidating hard edge.

The French are hardy walkers and adore fresh-air
outings, even though they are not into rough and
tumble sports or sweaty workouts. They have always
believed in "taking the waters," algae wraps, and
breathing in the mineral-filled air of their seaside spas.
They come from a strong agricultural tradition and
fill their diets with native fruits and vegetables, getting their protein from the nation's abundant dairy
products and famous cheeses. Enormous quantities of

"Both women and melons are best when fairly ripe."

Proverb

mineral water are consumed and domestic wines and champagnes take the place of hard liquor at their gala events. With less rigidity in the daily rigors it takes to become a financial tycoon and more emphasis on the art of living, such as the two-hour lunch, their stress level appears to be in the moderate zone. The high priority on enjoyment of life has helped the French to attain middle age with less wear and tear on the body's physical appearance. (Stress has noticeably taken its toll, however, on the generation that experienced the German occupation during World War II.)

Combine a stylish and emotionally mature woman enhanced by the secrets of French charm and seductiveness and you have a formidable competitor, even in a woman over fifty. After 50 or 60 years of nurturing their senses in the passionate and artistic traditions of their country, Frenchwomen are keenly adept in the art of nourishing those sensitivities in others.

As Marcel Proust beautifully describes in his admiration of a mature woman, "this woman may have done nothing singly spectacular except arouse by various magical summonses, a thousand components of tenderness, which she has brought together, united, eliminating all the spaces between them."

Proust goes on to say that men choose certain heroines "not necessarily for their age or beauty, but what really motivates the civilized man is the curiosity aroused by mystery and obstacle."

Aware of the comforting effects of loyal devotion and loving care, an experienced woman can attract a young man's regard with meaningful flattery and focused attention. The consoling aura of profound trust and delicate honesty bring men to rely on the presence of a favorite confidante.

Men do not usually reveal their soulful thoughts to another man as easily as they can to a woman, and it is said that nothing is so close to the truth as pillow talk. Once men learn to expose their inner thoughts with abandon and find that they can trust an attentive and tender listener, it is difficult for them to give up this refuge of cathartic discourse.

Frenchwomen with sophistication and experience have learned to wear lightly on a man's daily habits while they slowly and quietly weave a web around his existence Being creatures of habit, men like a peaceful and gratifying routine and are hesitant to change an accommodating situation unless it becomes unbearably painful or boring.

"Not to bore," say the French, "is the key ingredient to captivating a man's attention." To be able to stretch his imagination and lead him into new experiences without jolting his nerves, to be able to surprise him without shocking him, and to be able to tease him without laughing at him, keeps a lover addicted to the conductor of this orchestra of daily delights.

With little notice of their own age or the age of their "intended," ambitious courtesans who aim for men of high rank and nobility create a comforting and secure haven of wit, conversation, visual delights, soft lighting, appealing aromas, appropriate music and unexpected sensations to surround their target in an atmosphere of balanced elegance.

"At night faults
are unnoticed; any
woman can then pass
as a beauty."

Ovid
(43 B.C. - 18 A.D.)

These talents do not come without study, effort and a keen alertness. The skill lies in arranging the scene to look as if it is a completely natural part of one's daily living pattern, as if it all came about because the lovely creature was innately endowed with heavenly tendencies to live fully and lovingly. A man may go on a tangent with a tantalizing and youthful siren, but he is more likely to last a lifetime with a clever woman of any age who keeps him cerebrally enthralled and physically comfortable.

The magical techniques of Madame la Marquise de Pompadour kept the dashing King Louis XV fascinated for decades even after her interest in the sexual act had waned due to her poor health. Madame de Pompadour had unerring style, wit and grace and continued to fascinate the King and his intimate entourage until she died.

With all her goodness of heart, she was not without ambition for high places. From an early age she dedicated herself to the study and pursuit of quality and beauty. She did her homework well and after enchanting the King with her outstanding style and grace, she was able to hold him with her ability to create a miniature world of enchantment and peace, where her royal lover could learn the meaning of simple happiness in an easy informal atmosphere away from the formalities of the royal court. Even though she was well-read and intelligent, her conversation was gay, natural and unpretentious. She had the ability to adapt to each level of her guests, making every carefully chosen member of the group feel welcome and important.

Her friend, the philosopher Voltaire, saluted her without reservation when he said, "In you, all the arts, all taste and all ability to please are indeed united." He wrote in his memoirs that she had "gained the affection of the King by friendly intrigue and fearless conversation."

Louis XV who lived in constant view of the public and whose every thought, word and deed, no matter how trivial, personal or private, was observed, discussed and dissected, had never known a woman so seemingly natural. She combined the role of mistress, wise counselor and friend so well that he grew to rely on her candid opinions for the rest of her life.

This clever woman of a certain age knew the power of keeping a dynamic man interested and entertained, of knowing when enough was enough, and when to stop others who were beginning to irritate or bore him. Her exquisitely decorated private apartments in Versailles were a heavenly oasis for the harassed ruler where he could be alone with a delightful woman whom he trusted and loved, and no one, not even his children or his footman, had permission to enter that haven without an invitation.

The graceful, witty Pompadour was always full of fun and good humor, as well as brimming with freshness and amusing ideas. Even after the Marquise lost her exquisite figure, her ability to remain graceful, smell delicious, and never become a bore kept the king devoted to his trusted companion, although he had dalliances of the flesh with several other willing

"Shall I tell you
what makes love so
dangerous? 'Tis the
too high idea we are
apt to form it."

Ninon de L'Enclos
(1620 - 1705)

ladies who were barely out of their teens.

History book lessons extolling the talents of
famous French mistresses are eagerly read by the
young women in modern France wanting to learn
the art of seduction. When they are brought up with
positive attitudes concerning the methods of captivating and keeping men in their life stimulated and
amused, their talents can be honed to perfection and
the benefits do not necessarily wane with age.

Over three hundred years ago, Ninon de L'Enclos,
the famous courtesan of quality, took her last lover
at the age of 72. Her young admirer, a cousin of the
King of Sweden, was twenty at the time and didn't
care about the age of his mistress. He said, "Young
girls bore me, and I prefer the wisdom of experienced
women, especially my delicious, tender Ninon."

In 1693, when Ninon wrote to her
dear friend lamenting her advancing
years, he wrote to her in reply, "You
are more spiritual and intelligent than
the young Ninon; your life, my very
dear one, has been too brilliant for it
not to continue so to the end. What
ingratitude to be ashamed to name love,
when you owe all your charms and
graces to it. You were born to love all
your life. Lovers and gamblers have
something in common: once a true
lover, always a lover."

Frenchwomen heed their
heritage and their history lessons and do

not waste time moaning about the number of years they've spent on this earth, but get down to the business of living passionately, stylishly and gratefully.

pièce de résistance

As far back as 1370, Brantôme, the witty French chronicler, boasts about the amatory skills of Frenchwomen: "They have wisely learned from ardent research so many delightful ways, attractions, graces, positions, and exotic entertainments, while constantly eager to continue their knowledge, that I have heard foreigners say that making love with ladies from France is far superior to anything they have experienced."

The personal diaries of King Henry VIII of England tend to add credence to claims made about the special talents of French paramours. He was exuberant when writing about his delight in having a French mistress, "We hid sweetmeats in our private parts, to be extracted, as was our rule, only by the tongue, never by the fingers. We watched our reflections in reflecting mirrors, watching a hundred Henrys and Maries copulating in the mirror, that reflected the mirror, yet reflecting in another mirror. We wore masks and I was a savage and she was a Goddess of the Hunt. I entered her and we turned

"Desires are
nourished by
delays."

Proverb

the sandglass over and counted how many times we
could come to culmination, both together and separately...then I decked her naked body with my wife's
jewels and mounting her among the precious gems
felt the most adulterous of all. Expertly she swam
under me bringing me to la petite mort (the little
death) several times in succession. This is yet another
admirable French talent, as no femme fatale worthy of
her name is satisfied with only one orgasm—no, there
must be a series for both, the more the better. Such

exercises and flattery were only the beginning
of her artful French repertoire. There were
many other things that decency does not
permit me to record, even in my own private
book."

   Throughout the ages seductresses of France
have held tight to their international reputation as
fiery lovers whether they make a career of their
sexual expertise or choose to give freely for their own
pleasure or as a sincere act of impassionedness.

   The impression French women coyly relay to the
world is that they truly like to make love. One can
see it in their eyes, in their walk, and in their way of
dressing. If you have a discerning ear you should be
able to detect a voluptuous tone in their everyday
conversation when they order meat from the butcher, answer the phone, or greet a friend's husband on
the street.

   They are capable of vaguely transmitting the
notion that they would undress at any given moment
for a man who can make the circumstances interest-

ing enough to deserve the honor. This intoxicating readiness and simmering desire is a potent aphrodisiac when sniffed by most males possessing a healthy level of lust.

Smoldering body heat dangles impatiently along the sidewalks of Paris. The fantasy of sexual encounters lingers close to the surface of a man's libido when he is caught in the spell of this city's lavish beauty and a clever coquette can quickly bring this constantly stirring impulse into front and forward focus if she so chooses. The atmosphere of the French capital is famous as a feast for the senses, and the inhabitants do not try to hide their voracious appetites.

"Half—the most beautiful half—of life is hidden from those who have not loved passionately," advises Stendhal, the 19th Century author whom the French revere.

The people of France tend to agree with this romantic formula for love and desire, and for centuries they have been committed to the quest of the "love-journey" with all the thrills and dangers along the bumpy pursuit.

"Carnality," wrote the 16th Century Francis Bacon, "is imprinted upon the spirit of man by an innate inward instinct." Frenchwomen are world-class champions at deciphering this shadowy language of lustful yearning. They have developed through practice as well as their own self-interest, a keen sense in detecting when a man is ripe for amorous adventures.

Research cannot be precise on levels of sexual longing; however, one can surmise from the huge bulk of

> "They love too much that die for love."
>
> Proverb

sensuous literature, architecture and visual arts created in the past millennium that profuse energy has been ignited by love spurts and carnal explosions.

"The French have the proper latitude and attitude for love. At their best they are lucid, literate, and tolerant, and they are blessed with an unguilty sense of pleasure. The American author, James Barry, an admitted Francophile, writes, "If I had to hazard a definition of French sexuality, I would say it is sensuality sharpened by intellectuality."

Although a Parisian damsel may hint at a copious capacity for amour, she does not leave her boudoir door wide open for suitors to enter at will. She is far too savvy about the thrill that men derive from the chase and the gratification of the final conquest. Gamesmanship is paramount in most aspects of French life and capturing the heart is an all-time favorite sport.

If the situation and time permit, an experienced player will produce an entertaining melodrama for the target of her desire, with all the props of a live theatrical performance—the stage, the overture, the costumes, the sound effects, the lighting, and the scenery. The leading lady will then play out the suspense, the conflict and the surrender leading to the final act. If the performance has gone well, both the hero and the heroine are rewarded with the coveted burst of rapture and immediate demands for encores.

Even though a continental glamour queen is perfectly capable of controlling the entire production herself, she adroitly keeps the spotlight on the male

star and makes certain that he gathers all the honors
in the final bow.

A French temptress has few barriers about sexual
activities and knows better than to give the impression that a lover's ardent advances are an inconve-
nience. She is aware that men fantasize about making
love in unlikely places during stolen moments of the
day or night. Chance and surprise occurrences of copulation fuse well with the character of a true "seductress," who knows that the ever-brewing testosterone
level flows more freely in unexpected situations
rather than on a routine or demanded schedule. Her
tact or tenderness in this circumstance may depend
on the interest she has in the pursuer or what he has
to offer, but usually a French lady will leave a man's
ego unbruised whether she goes through with the
ultimate request or leaves him panting with hope for
another opportunity in the future.

"Quickie" or "sudden sex" is not of great interest
among continental lovers. They prefer their partners
to take time for creativeness in love-making and
elaborate efforts are practiced by French mistresses to
keep the script and scenery fresh. (This is not to say
that any Latin-blooded male would not jump on the
opportunity for a chance encounter if he could still
get to his next appointment on time.)

Sophisticated love scenarios, making use of intellectuality, finesse, surprise, and originality to pump up
strength in the age-old mating game, are required to
titillate the Gallic imagination. Satire, wit, innuendos
and cleverness are as necessary as physical agility for

"Men, in
general, are but
great children."

Napoleon
Bonaparte

(1769-1821)

winning top honors.

Enormous curiosity has kept the French open to
sexual variation, deviations and experimentation. It
is not often that they speak of "sexual perversion,"
as very few carnal acts are considered abnormal in
this nation of glorified body language. They remain
loyal to their hard earned civil rights, however, and
insist that any adventurous sexual acts do not infringe
upon the comfort or health of other citizens.

Apparently, the commonplace position of copulation with the male on top is considered too unimagi-
native for Latin libertines. Love-making is the one
activity that inspires the French to exercise vigorously,
using athletic positions from the rear, upside-down,
standing up, from the side and swinging from spe-
cially designed furniture. One unique piece from the
18th Century recently went on the block at Drouet,
the well-known Paris auction house. The chair-like
contraption was such a confused puzzle of foot rests,
head holders, steps and cushioned movable parts that
it would take a nimble and ingenious lover to take
full advantage of it. The frantic bidding at high stakes
had imaginations in the room soaring with exotic
notions.

Continental men have little interest in having
their buttocks spanked, leaving that fantasy to their
English neighbors, who grew up receiving blows from
a paddle in boys' schools. The French are a more oral
nation, using their mouths for numerous pleasures in
pontificating, singing, eating, kissing, biting, sucking,
and tasting every precious part of a juicy love feast.

Generally Frenchmen are not aroused by brutality or torture, except in the sado-masochistic groups. It is quite acceptable, however, in polite society to respect a lady who can deliver a resounding slap in the face to someone who has pushed bad manners to the limit.

In contrast to the involved love drama which requires time and mental effort, many men can be made happy with a mindless adventure of total abandon with a playful prostitute. This furtive fantasy offers a man the ultimate freedom from commitment and responsibility and stirs up the exhilarating elements of secrecy, danger and a taste of the forbidden.

From the era of its location as a Roman campsite to the present day, Paris has hosted a hotbed of debauchery, and "French Madams" have been famous for creating tempting and fanciful brothels. Even today the provincial villages and country hamlets, as well as Paris, maintain a special nonchalance toward local "parlors of pleasure." The tolerance for this facet of life is merely another clue to understanding the realistic attitude of the pragmatic French personality.

Molière, Dumas, Flaubert, Zola, Baudelaire, Fragonard, Manet, Degas, Lautrec, Picasso and scores of other geniuses have offered us novels, paintings, diaries, operas and plays describing "houses of joy" and "ladies of easy virtue."

Writers and artists have dwelled upon the decadent plight, as well as the delicious delights of prostitutes and their deeds since civilization began. Judging from the abundance of lascivious material left to us by famous artists in written word and on canvas, one

"When she raises her eyelids, it's as if she's taking off all her clothes."

Colette
(1873-1954)

hesitates to guess at the even more lewd cravings that go on among the depraved folks.

In the 1860's Charles Baudelaire wrote from personal experience, "The prostitute represents the unconsciousness which allows us to put aside our responsibilities...forgetting is the core of this particular gratification of desire."

Without asking for explanations, promises, etiquette, decorum or conversation, bold and brassy merchants of sexual favors are willing to strike a bargain for any type of doable deed that a client requests. One can live out the fantasy of dirty talk, staring, hanging from a trapeze, rolling in whipped cream, or being paddled with an instrument of his choice—all with minimum discussion once the fee is paid. This noncommittal source of sin can propel a purging gush of fluid frustration for one who is hounded in his conventional lifestyle with constant demands on his time, brain and psyche.

Although there are endless opportunities for non-commercial sexual experiences in France, energetic French harlots have managed to keep their ancient vocation alive and active, even through they complain about a deflated bottom line lately due to the AIDS scare. Rising to the need of its citizens' safety, the French government offers regular health exams free-of-charge to the ladies who are in the business of selling love .

Elite social strata of French society have been known to enlist "experts of the flesh" to initiate their adolescent boys into the mysteries of adult sexuality. The ritual is decorously carried out by approved courtesans, ladies' maids or the adept friends of concerned family members.

In former times, the royal family in power had to see to it that the heir-apparent was introduced to heterosexual habits before the male dandies of the court sneaked into his bedchamber. It was imperative to establish that the son of the king had the functioning tools to propagate heirs to the throne. The dauphin's sexual education usually began when he was about 12 or 13 years old and there was always a frenzy of intense interviews to select the most qualified and sensitive soul to perform the rites of puberty.

History books record several instances of these important introductions into manhood. In 1653, a close friend of Louis XIV's mother was given an elegant mansion in gratitude for her services to the 15 year old future king. The helpful Madame Catherine de Beauvais and her husband Pierre were given noble titles and the beautiful Hotel de Beauvais in Paris which stills stands on the Rue François Miron near the Seine. The rewards were evidently well earned, for it is said that Louis XIV went on to enjoy an enormous appetite for romping with a great variety of ladies, as well as his Queen, and sired numerous children, both legitimate and otherwise.

In the current world of instant communication, it is hardly necessary to encourage early sexual skills among young people due to their heighten awareness and exposure to electronically relayed information. And even though France is considered a predomi-

nately Catholic nation, birth control materials are readily available, thus allowing a new comfort zone in liberated lovemaking.

There have been great changes in the love manners of Frenchwomen since the Middle Ages when the Roman Catholic Church made it necessary to disguise any pleasure connected with dutiful procreation. Before 1200 the joys of physical unions were kept in the shadows of secret corners and under the cover of night, spoken about only in guarded whispers.

Beginning in the 1300s when the age of gallant knights, troubadours, and musketeers galloped upon the French countryside, new feelings about romance and its pleasures came into play. Romantic poetry, playful songs, tender dancing and suggestive skits did much to unveil the pent-up yearnings of the robust and sensual Franks.

The natural progression of this gratifying enlightenment was quick to catch on after the grim Dark Ages and continued at a rapid pace until the present day when the average Frenchwoman appears openly comfortable about discussing her basic cravings as well as displaying her well-cared for body.

The contemporary Frenchwoman has a healthy attitude about physical love and individual sexual preferences and can discuss with aplomb topics that concern bisexuality, masturbation, body organs, love triangles, sex scandals, and so on. The Gallic nation as a whole reacts with amusement to the Puritanical reactions of Americans to adultery, homosexuality, nudity and the amorous affairs of their public officials.

The sensitivities of French schoolgirls have an ideal training ground for early awareness in a country where countless layers of visual and sensual entice-ments bombard the human spirit in the lusciousness of the cultural climate. The open and frank treatment of human anatomy and its passionate responses in French art, literature, and movies are available to chil-dren in France without embarrassment, letting them grow up with a natural acceptance of their bodies and sexuality.

The young women grow up in the midst of proud-ly groomed parks and avenues, the aromatic smells of creative cuisine, tender contact at festive family gatherings, the lush tones of a romance language, a sparkling national history, and an ever-present alert-ness to style—an atmosphere that breeds a richness of sensuality. "The appetite grows by eating," writes Rabelais.

There is very little argument, even among today's feminist movement, that the art of womanliness is one of the precious pleasures that enriches the qual-ity of life. The opportunity to reap the rewards of femininity is rarely resisted by the most powerful and successful women in France's working force. A French female is as prideful of her gifts of gender as a man is of his "family jewels."

In fact both men and women in France have an air of such contentment about their wealth of talent and tools for amour that it comes as no surprise that they take every opportunity to exhibit these abilities

in imaginative ways. To their credit the ingredient
that renders this smug attitude of sexual superiority
tolerable to themselves and the rest of the world is a
humorous and non-serious approach to lovemaking.
Past history is too ingrained in the French psyche to
blindly believe in the permanence of passionate love.

The acceptance level in France for personal gratification games and theatrics continues to fascinate
world audiences who exist in the more puritan or
hypocritical societies of the world. The French are
pleased as well as amused about their reputation as
champions of love and romance. Smug smiles greet
the widely circulated tales of their excessive bed frol-
ics as they bask in the beauty of Paris, the grand incu-
bator of sensual delights.

Parisians proudly refer to their capital as "the city
of light and love;" they think of it as a giant theatrical
stage for extraordinary sensations of the mind and of
the flesh. Law makers and the local inhabitants take
little notice concerning the boundaries of erotic practices as long as there is adult consent and the antics
do not disturb public property or neighborhood sensitivities.

Although I confess that I have not been privy to
the physical repertoire of French lovers, I have wit-
nessed their tantalizing conversation. In the guise of
intelligent discussions, both men and women feel free
to spice up their discourse with tidbits on fellatio,
cunnilingus, copraphilia, tribadism, zoophilia, voyeur-
ism and bisexuality.

One of the subtle, yet disarming, devices of proper

French grand dames is their talent to ignite men to
fervent mental wanderings and then listen attentively
without displaying any aversion, to their fantasies.
Whether such imaginary escapades will actually
become a reality is another story; however, most men
admit to having vicarious thrills when listened to
with thoughtful attention when they describe their
secret sexual dreams.

Seasoned coquettes are well-versed in the old stand-
bys that have seduced men throughout the ages: flattery, attention, focus, encouragement, glamour, wit,
novelty in lovemaking, and the ability to convince a
man of his superior and unique "manliness." A clever
courtesan usually does not lower herself to beg for
commitment or everlasting love, but will put more
effort into intriguing her lover to the extent that his
interests are sufficiently satisfied. She continually
relays the illusion of being content with "these precious moments" in life when she is with her true love,
with no cares of before and after.

Putting into play their expert intuitive skills, sensual talents, and powerful self-confidence while frolicking in a fluffy bed chamber has been the inimitable
premise from which Frenchwomen have continuously cast a hypnotic spell over their countrymen. Most
Frenchmen will readily admit that the women of
their nation have proceeded to quietly rule the nation
from the shadows of satin sheets.

"Everything depends on her," said Jean-Jacques
Rousseau in 1750, "nothing is done except by her or
for her."

> "No one knows
> like a woman
> how to say
> things which
> are at once
> gentle and
> deep."
>
> Victor Hugo
> (1802-1885)

As for listing all the recipes for French lovemaking variations, positions, and contraptions, that is not my intent, as doubling this tome would hardly cover the gamut. Graphic manuals on the subject are so readily available in France that I prefer not to plagiarize text and sketches that may well limit the circulation of this book to adult bookstores.

Suffice to say that the Franks have been experimenting with the art of love for two millenniums and have heard it all and are willing to try it all. The English limerick that goes, "The French they are a funny race, they fight with their feet and fuck with their face," is much too simplified to describe the complicated and creative French people. Their hunger for novelty and their voracious curiosity have lead them to discoveries that most Puritanical Americans hesitate to think of or explore. The imaginative French are not hampered in their thinking by layers of guilt or self-consciousness.

France is thought of as the mecca of intellectual snobs where learning is a powerful motivator; however, the French are not prudish about what subjects their wealth of knowledge covers. They have the imaginations, the resources, the history, the desire, and the setting to be world-class contenders in the game of love.

PHOTO CREDITS
All efforts have been made to accurately credit the images used in this book. Corrections received after publication will be added to subsequent editions.

Cover and p. 8, *Nude on a Sofa (Reclining Girl)*, François Boucher, 1752, oil on canvas, Pinakothek at Munich.

p. 13, Hulton Getty Collection
p. 14, *Leda and the Swan*, François Boucher, 1741
p. 18, Hulton Getty Collection
p. 20, Hulton Getty Collection
p. 23, Hulton Getty Collection
p. 24, Hulton Getty Collection
p. 28, *The Toilet of Venus*, François Boucher, 1751, oil on canvas,
The Metropolitan Museum of Art, New York.
p. 31, *Diane de Poitiers*, François Clouet, 1571, wood,
The National Gallery of Art at Washington D.C.
p. 32, *Portrait of Mary of Burgundy*, unknown artist, (Flemish) late 15th Century,
panel painting, Musée Condé at Chantilly
p. 37, *Portrait of Madame Roger Jourdain*, Albert Besnard, 1886, oil on canvas,
Musée d'Orsay in Paris.
p. 42, *The Bolt (Le Verrou)*, Jean-Honoré Fragonard, c. 1778, oil on canvas,
Musee du Louvre, Paris
p. 54, *Two Women Holding Flowers*, Fernand Léger, 1954, Tate Gallery, London.
p. 62, *Madame de Loynes*, Eugène-Emmanuel Amaury-Duval, 1862, oil on canvas,
Musée d'Orsay at Paris.
p. 65, *The Love Letter*, Jean-Honoré Fragonard, 1770s, oil on canvas,
Metropolitan Museum of Art, New York.
p. 66, Hulton Getty Collection
p. 70, Hulton Getty Collection
p. 75, Hulton Getty Collection
p. 79, Hulton Getty Collection
p. 80, Hulton Getty Collection
p. 84, *The Melun Diptych* (detail featuring The Virgin and Child), Jean Fouquet (or Foucquet),
1453-54, Musée de l'Hospice at Villeneuve-les-Avignon.
p. 87, *The Empress Eugénie*, Franz-Xaver Winterhalter, 1854, oil on canvas,
Metropolitan Museum of Art, New York.
p. 89, Liane de Pougy, unknown
p. 92, *Young Woman Ironing*, Louis Léopold Boilly, 1800, Museum of Fine Arts, Boston.
p. 96, Hulton Getty Collection
p. 102, *The Wait*, Jean Béraud, undated, oil on canvas, Musée d'Orsay at Paris.
p. 104, Hulton Getty Collection
p. 107, Hulton Getty Collection
p. 108, Hulton Getty Collection
p. 111, Hulton Getty Collection
p. 112, *Portrait of Madame Guillaume*, André Derain, 1928, Musée de l'Orangerie, Paris.
p. 117, Hulton Getty Collection
p. 120, Hulton Getty Collection
p. 124, *The Birth of Venus*, Alexandré Cabanel, 1863, Musée d'Orsay at Paris.
p. 125, Hulton Getty Collection
p. 131, Hulton Getty Collection

Back cover, Hulton Getty Collection